REALISM RESCUED

REALISM RESCUED

How Scientific Progress Is Possible

Jerrold L. Aronson

Rom Harré

Eileen Cornell Way

Open Court

Chicago and La Salle, Illinois

Published by arrangement with Gerald Duckworth & Co. Ltd., London.

First printing 1995

Printed and bound in the United States of America.

Library of Congress Cataloging-in-Publication Data

Aronson, Jerrold L., 1940–
    Realism rescued : how scientific progress is possible / Jerrold L. Aronson, Rom Harré, and Eileen Cornell Way.
        p.   cm.
    Includes bibliographical references and index.
    ISBN 0-8126-9288-8. — ISBN 0-8126-9289-6 (pbk.)
    1. Realism. 2. Science—Methodology. 3. Research—Methodology.
I. Harré, Rom. II. Way, Eileen Cornell. III. Title.
Q175.32.R42A76   1995
507.2—dc20   94-47940
                                                             CIP

Contents

Preface

The problem of finding a definitive series of analyses and arguments that will serve as a final and uncontrovertible defence of an adequate account of scientific realism has occupied the three of us for many years. Our discussions have been made possible in large part by the support given to a long series of minicourses in the philosophy of science at SUNY Binghamton. Early versions of some of the chapters were first presented at the Inter-University Centre at Dubrovnik, and benefited greatly from the robust atmosphere of debate amongst the members of the Easter courses. We are grateful to Bill Newton-Smith, Michael Redhead, Ian Aitchison, Jerry Vision and many others for gently but firmly reminding us of the shortcomings of some of our earlier attempts.

Is the dragon of anti-realism finally dead? We doubt it. However we do flatter ourselves that when it re-emerges it will have an entirely new shape.

A deadly virus infected the disks on which our text was taking final form. We are grateful to Lin Barnetson for mounting a brilliant and successful rescue operation.

There is no 'senior author' for this work. Our names are listed on the title page in alphabetical order.

Linacre College, Oxford.
Psychology Department, Georgetown University.
Program in Philosophy and Computers and Systems Science, Philosophy Department, Binghamton University.

'In time one comes to revise all views,
just as one comes to see that very little
is "pure" anything.'

A.N. Wilson, *Incline our hearts*

CHAPTER ONE

The Realism Debates

1. Introduction: the weakness of 'modest realism'

The defence of scientific realism has had to be undertaken afresh from time to time. Sceptics find new grounds for their attacks on the pretensions of the scientific community to be giving an ever more accurate and unbiased account of the natural world. Under the pressures of more and more sophisticated sceptical arguments the doctrine of scientific realism has become progressively more refined and finely differentiated. Sometimes the efforts of realists to refine their position have taken a wrong direction. We believe that some of the defensive strategies realists have adopted are mistaken. We shall demonstrate that it is not the best strategy to emphasise that realism is best characterised as a metaphysical doctrine first and foremost, and to relegate semantic and epistemic issues to the status of more secondary problems. It has been suggested that if the most impressive recent attacks on realism have focused on the latter they are beside the point. Anti-realists have been accused of arguing against a 'straw man', of attacking a cluster of doctrines that are not part of a well-thought-out realism. Eliminating many of the arguments against realism by showing that they are attacking claims which are not essential to the realist position is, indeed, a tempting strategy.

Here are some examples of this strategy at work. Some anti-realists argue that the history of science has brought to light numerous cases where the pragmatic success of a theory in predicting phenomena does not indicate that it is getting closer to the truth, increasing in verisimilitude. This has been called the 'meta-induction argument'. Others have claimed that scientific progress can be defined and accounted for without having to appeal to the idea of verisimilitude at all. Finally, many anti-realists maintain that defending realism by claiming that it provides the only plausible explanation of scientific progress simply begs the question. It presuppposes that we have an independent criterion for discerning that progress. In response to this onslaught, some realists have tried to recast their philosophy in such a way as to avoid these criticisms, by making the doctrine of realism more modest but retaining its essential features. While some (Margolis, 1985) have given up the idea that the substantive terms of a theory should be taken to refer to real entities and states of affairs existing independently of the observer in favour of a neo-pragmatism, others (Newton-Smith, 1990) have given up the requirement that the ultimate criterion of realism is that theories be true or false. At the worst these strategies amount to no more than a limiting of realism to the assertion that there exists a mind-independent world which is *somehow* related to the techniques and discourses of scientific communities. According to this view, the epistemological aspects of the doctrine of scientific realism are to be dropped, for they are nothing but hostages to fortune, and inessential to realism. If they cannot be defended against the attacks of sceptics they had best be abandoned. Likewise, the notion of degrees of truth through which one approach to scientific progress has been defined has been much criticised. Again the modest realist strategy has been to abandon this idea as well, as unnecessary to characterising the heart of scientific realism.

We agree that many of the problems associated with fending off these recent anti-realist attacks result from a failure to separate metaphysical, semantical and epistemological issues, and that attempts to refine and make more precise the true nature of the realist doctrine are certainly justified. However, we are also convinced that some of these refinements have led to a watering down of realism to the point that many anti-realists can claim that the weakened version of realism is perfectly compatible with the main tenets of anti-realism.

But there are other things that disturb us about attempts at revising realism by limiting it in this way. If scientific realism is first and foremost a metaphysical doctrine, as Devitt (1984) claims, it is not a very interesting one. All it says is that there is a mind-independent world, consisting of different types or kinds of things. The proponents of this view never go into what it means to be a type of thing or how different types are related to one another. In addition to this, the relationship between theories and the articulated parts of this so-called mind-independent world is not spelled out. If the terms of a theory do not refer to mind-independent entities how does theory reach out to reality? For example, what parts or aspects of the world is a particular theory *about*? If theories are neither true nor false how is it that some theories are better related to the world than others? Even more important, if realism is to be stripped of truth, verisimilitude and other concepts traditionally associated with it, how is it related to the many other features that realism must include besides truth and verisimilitude? What is the nature of scientific progress? Why are models indispensable? What is the nature of laws and their associated counterfactuals? And so on. In other words, if realism is just the bare assertion that there is a mind-independent world but says nothing about the nature of that world nor explains how other aspects of the discourse and practice of science fit into such a view, such a version of realism is too impoverished to be of interest even as a metaphysical doctrine.

2. What is at issue between realists and anti-realists?

Let us now try to look more deeply into the background assumptions of the participants in the debate. It has been customary for philosophers to take 'science' as something made concrete as discourses: that is, as journal articles, text books, monographs and lectures. It would then be natural to interpret verisimilitude in terms of the relative truth and falsity of the propositions expressed by the statements that constitute those scientific discourses. Much of the recent realist/antirealist debate has occurred in the context of this interpretation of verisimilitude. But there is another way in which one can think of the verisimilitude of science. 'Science' also takes concrete form in models and experimental procedures. Models are real or imagined representations and analogues of naturally occurring entities, structures and processes. Experimental procedures not only lead to observable results but involve the manipulation of substances and entities which human beings are unable to observe.

Most scientific discourse is not about the natural world but about representations of selected aspects of that world. Our conceptions of what nature is are mediated by our representations of nature in models, which, as we shall see, are subject to certain important constraints. Constraints on our best representations of naturally occurring structures and processes mostly reflect historical conditions for the intelligibility of those representations and the experimental procedures we have devised for manipulating them. We shall be developing a semiformal theory of those constraints in terms of type-hierarchies. The verisimilitude of science from this point of view is to be assessed by attention to the degree of match or mismatch between models and what they represent. How is this to be achieved, if all we have are representations? To this fundamental question we believe we can offer an original and plausible answer.

In turning away from a form of realism based on the verisimilitude of discourses, which requires a solution to the perennial problem of adequately characterising propositional truth, to a doctrine based on the verisimilitude of models, in which the root idea is that of pictorial truth, we shed the burden of one range of philosophical problems at the cost of taking up another. Our aim in this book is to show how this shift of attention facilitates the defence of a strong form of scientific realism in which notions like 'law' and 'progress' have a well-defined place.

What we are seeking is a notion of realism that shows us how all these associated doctrines fit together. As in old-fashioned realism, we seek unification. The key lies in a proper understanding of what theories are and what they enable us to do. The key to the key, so to say, is the development of an adequate way of representing what theories are. We shall explain and defend the view that the vast majority of scientific theories denote chunks or segments of ordered systems of natural kinds. This view is hardly new, but we believe it has never before been presented in the right degree of technical detail. Furthermore we hope to show that the more fundamental the theory, the greater the chunk or segment of a system of natural kinds the theory, as a whole, denotes. These chunks are captured or represented by sections of type-hierarchies. A type-hierarchy is a device invented by researchers in artificial intelligence, and it will play a central role in our representations of theories.

It is all very well to claim that the type-hierarchies expressing the common ontology of a family of theories denote a segment or chunk of a system of natural kinds. But before we can expect that idea to carry conviction we must give an account of exactly what these type-hierarchies represent. For example, we must address the question as to what is a natural kind? How are natural kinds related? In particular, how is a more specific natural kind like RED PINE related to its more general supertype, TREE? And how do particulars enter into the philosophical account of science? How is it that I know a great deal about the tree in my garden if I know that it instantiates the type *Red Pine*? We will learn in the next chapter that answering these questions involves making numerical identity both of individuals and and of properties basic or primitive, that is undefined ontological categories in our system. But doesn't this beg all the questions about the concept of 'type' that have troubled philosophers since the platonic universal first bothered Aristotle? Our answer is essentially pragmatic. It is a commonplace of metaphysical debate that not every concept in a system can be explicated. At some point the root ideas are just displayed. It has been famously said that what cannot be said can be shown. We shall show how by a wise choice of primitives or root ideas a convincing account of science can be constructed.

3. An outline of our approach

One way to 'test' this ontology would be to convince the reader that such a view best makes sense of the other doctrines associated with realism. We shall show that it makes clear how models work, that it provides a semantics for some of the most problematic concepts of the old framework, such as 'truth' and 'verisimilitude', and finally that it offers far more satisfactory resolutions of some of the problems that proved so intractable in the old metaphysical context: for instance, the problem of understanding counterfactuals, and many others. Our central thesis, then, is that the above doctrines that the revisionists of realism want to keep separate from the central metaphysical doctrine are really constitutive of it.

We submit that viewing nature as an ordering of natural kinds, represented by type-hierarchies, leads to a new type of metaphysics. Instead of speaking of isolated substances and their properties, we speak of systems where the internal relations among properties determine the system as being of a particular type, captured by giving it a specific location in the type-hierarchy. From the point of the human observer or manipulator ascriptions of these properties must always take the form of dispositions. It is the very same location in an ordering of natural kinds that enables systems, in the above sense, to serve as models. In other words, ontological atomism is replaced by global-ontological relationalism. And here we will learn one way in which this particular metaphysical doctrine has serious ramifications for the epistemology of science. We cannot make categorical or counterfactual predictions ('What will happen when ...' or 'What would happen were ...') until we first determine the specific nature of the system with which we are dealing. The atomistic, non-contextual initial conditions of the old logicist or deductive-nomological approach are to be replaced by locating a system in a type-hierarchy. There are many type-hierarchies corresponding to many different orderings of natural kinds. In which hierarchy a system is to be located is a function of context. This is worked out in detail in the course of the book.

Another outcome of this metaphysics, which will be developed later in the book, is that the traditional ontological primacy of atomistic and categorical properties over relational and dispositional properties is rejected, but not in favour of a wholesale shift to an ontology that (paradoxically) recognises only the reality of possibilities. According to our position, there is no difference between the system's being of a certain type and its having a specific range of dispositional properties. All the possibilities are contained within the system, so to speak, in virtue of the fact that it is of that particular type. Perhaps this view can be traced to Bohr, Popper or even Aristotle, but the major source of the idea as we present it here is from the notion that nature collects properties into an underlying ordering of natural kinds.

In most of this book we show how such a metaphysics has a profound effect on semantics. In the spirit of Wittgensteinian philosophy, the unit of meaning is not the proposition but a chunk of a hierarchy (or a part of a 'model of the world') picked out by the language games that are proper within a given context. What we have, here, is an ontosemantics. What is meant, in part, is explicated in terms of the workings of the cognitive mechanisms realised in scientific discourse. These mechanisms involve operations on a type-hierarchy that represents the models of the world respectively held by the participants in the communicative network. Understanding what people mean, then, requires an understanding, sharing or elucidating of their picture or model of the world, no matter how crude or sophisticated it may be. Naturally the same goes for understanding their theories.

4. Why logicism must be abandoned

We did not arrive at this position by thinking of scientific language as a calculus or an inference engine, with a resultant clear separation between literal and figurative language, in the manner of traditional positivist and logicist philosophers. Ironically we are seeing scientific discourse through the eyes of metaphor, just in order to grasp its literal sense. To understand the actual cognitive mechanisms of science, we must first place figurative language on a equal footing with the literal. It has recently become fashionable to jettison the 'literal/metaphorical' terminology to express the difference between non-figurative and figurative uses of words. However, we find it convenient to retain these expressions, though we do not subscribe to the old view that if words do not correspond to something real they are merely being used decoratively. The cognitive mechanisms through which 'science' is constituted are represented by a variety of operations on a type-hierarchy, each of equal status with any other. Viewing things this way will make it easy to understand that the cognitive mechanisms underlying metaphorical thinking and scientific modelling are to all intents and purposes the same. Science imitates art and *vice versa*.

The dominant tradition in philosophy of science has logic and formal philosophy of language driving any analysis of scientific theory. Until now it has been ideal language philosophy or some variant of symbolic logic (first-order predicate calculus with identity, set theory etc.) which has been the main resource for trying to capture the essence of the scientific-literal uses of language. Until recently it appeared that Wittgensteinian insights into how language actually worked were not amenable to formal treatments. Hence what recourse did philosophers of science in a search of formal transparency have if they could not come up with a formal system that did justice to the subtleties of language? It was symbolic logic and set theory or nothing. However, recent developments in artificial intelligence, especially in the areas of knowledge representation and natural language processing, led to the development of a new range of tools that seem to be just what is required to achieve an unproblematic analysis at the highest level of abstraction by displaying inherent formal structures that capture the features of natural language that have previously escaped analysis, features like context and open-textured meaning. But the application of these structures is first and foremost motivated by an understanding of language which is not prejudiced by a commitment to symbolic logic. In other words, if we are to rescue realism, we must abandon our logicist ways and think of language, including scientific language, in an entirely new light.

We have argued elsewhere that theories are metaphysical systems in disguise, that explanation takes place by identifying independent phenomena with aspects of a common ontology. So, theories are not to be thought of as sets of propositions, though they can be expressed propositionally. Rather, they are models, embedded in type-hierarchies, chunks of orderings of natural kinds. While we agree with Giere that theories are best thought of as families of models, indeed we have been arguing for this view for more than thirty years(!), these models are just the tip of the iceberg, for they occur at the lower levels of the hierarchy. In fact it is their relative locations at the lowest level of type-hierarchies that make systems usable as models in the first place. This is because the type-hierarchy is responsible for generating the crucial, relative similarity relationships between systems, upon which the use of some system as a model, that is an abstraction from, idealisation of or analogue to some other system, depends. Again, working with models scientists are not just comparing properties of things in an atomistic fashion but are making similarity comparisons between *types of systems* within a given context. Seeing models in this perspective will go a long way to show why they are an indispensable feature of scientific theories.

Suppose we concede, though we shall show that there is

reason to think the concession unnecessary, that whatever we have just said about the nature of theories, models, ordered structures of natural kinds, type-hierarchies, and so on, can always be expressed using the propositions of predicate calculus or set theory. This would not make a theory a set of propositions, any more than using a proposition to express my desire to eat a banana makes my desire a proposition. So, if a logicistically-minded philosopher were to translate what we claim a theory is into a set of propositions, the content of these propositions still consists of orderings of natural kinds, models of the world, etc., not sets of propositions. We have argued elsewhere (Harré, 1986) that at any moment in the development of a family of theories, united by their common ontology, the state of knowledge at that point can be (partially) represented by a set of propositions. We usually call these sets of propositions 'text books'. This is indeed an elementary point. But the logicist approach to the problems of understanding science remains so powerful that this distinction is easily glossed over by its adherents. What we are seeking, in part, are the cognitive mechanisms underlying theorising; we are not in the least concerned with translating them into a formal language unless there is a natural motivation for doing so. Why bother to translate these results into another and more problematic formal language if they are already expressed in a naturally motivated knowledge-representation system, especially if we run the risk of losing something in the translation?

5. Salvaging the concepts of truth and verisimilitude for science

We believe that there is an intrinsic connection between orderings of natural kinds, type-hierarchies and model systems, on the one hand, and truth and verisimilitude on the other. We intend to show that attempts to formulate scientific realism without some concept of truth or verisimilitude are misguided. Everything depends on what we take those famously tendentious concepts to be, *in this context*. The very mechanism underlying realist approaches to theories actually serves to generate a kind of truth and verisimilitude, the kind that counts in science. Any full-blown realistic account of science and scientific theories has truth and all its trappings built in. The argument for this is very simple. The structure of natural kinds generates the similarities required for one system to be a model of another. How well a theoretical system models the real system determines the verisimilitude of a theory. According to this scheme, truth is not to be thought of as a correspondence between a proposition and the world but, instead, as a limiting case of verisimilitude. The truth of a theory occurs when the chunk of the hierarchy picked out by the theory exactly resembles the actual hierarchy. We have reversed primitive or basic epistemic concepts here. Traditional theories of verisimilitude or approximate truth use the truth of a proposition and sets of proposition as a basic unit in trying to construct some sort of measure of the distance any given theory lies from the truth. According to our scheme the concepts of truth and verisimilitude must be ranked in just the reverse order. If truth is a limiting case of verisimilitude, we must first understand what verisimilitude is in order to understand what truth is. This means, however, that the semantic cross, 'How are theories related to the world?', must be borne anyway. Any realist account of science must therefore bring truth and verisimilitude back into the fold, but only in the right way.

6. An inductive strategy for assessing verisimilitude

The general thesis of scientific realism, be it expressed in terms of the truth of propositions or of the verisimilitude of pictures and models, comprehends a number of subtheses and interpretative versions which need to be distinguished clearly at the outset of our enquiry. There are the cluster of 'ontosemantic' questions: what can it mean to say that one theory is nearer to or further from the truth than another, has greater or lesser verisimilitude, than a rival in the same field of enquiry? These questions must not be run into or elided with a quite different cluster of epistemological problems. How can we tell which of a pair of rival theories is nearer to or further from the truth? Yet it is also obvious that these groups of questions are not wholly independent of one another.

How are these clusters of questions connected? Traditionally difficulties in answering the latter have been taken as a good reason for taking up a sceptical attitude to the former. If there is no obvious and defensible way of telling which of a pair of rivals is nearer to or further from the truth, then the very idea of 'verisimilitude' is at best empty and at worst incoherent. Bhaskar (1973) has identified this line of argument as the demonstration of the 'epistemic fallacy'. We share his view that the sceptical inference is unwarranted. Epistemic scepticism does not entail ontosemantic scepticism. With the analysis and defence of a concept of verisimilitude and its derivative 'truth', as we have sketched these above in the ontosemantic context, in hand, we shall develop an answer to epistemic scepticism. We shall show how it is possible to treat the problem of choosing between rival philosophical theories, realism or scepticism, as itself an empirical question. Our approach has an ancestor in the well-known 'argument to the best explanation', but differs from it in a very fundamental way. According to that argument there is a parallel to be drawn between the way we use pragmatic success to choose among rival theories and the pragmatic success of science in general as a ground for a general realism. According to Boyd (1984) and Putnam (1984) the increase of verisimilitude of science as a whole is the only way we can make sense of the idea of scientific progress. Anti-realists have attacked this claim in a rather devastating way. Besides coming up with ways of explaining progress without having to postulate verisimilitude, they have also pointed out, correctly, we think, that this application of historical evidence to support the claim for progress as an inference to the best explanation actually presupposes a connection between what it is to be a good explanation and its truth or verisimilitude. Thus, this form of the inductive justification of realism begs the question.

Accepting the above anti-realist criticism, we approach the justification of realism differently. The trick is to establish the connection between verisimilitude and progress empirically, by means of an inductive inference without begging the question of what counts as a good theory. Both Laudan (1981) and van Fraasen (1980) accept the rationality and indispensability of induction in science. They are not Humean sceptics. If we are to establish the relationship between improved predictions and truth proximity on the basis of inductive reasoning, then the strength of the induction is only as good as the sample class of experiments we use as evidence – for example, it will depend on how unbiased these cases are and how well they represent the situation that actually exists in science. In other words there are certain canons of testing that must be satisfied if this is to be a good induction. But this is precisely what Laudan demands in his account of scientific progress, viz. we explain progress in terms of those theories that independently meet the rigours of experimental testing. So, by Laudan's very own standards, if the experimental results establish a connection between success and verisimilitude, and if the sample class is representative or unbiased, then the inductive inference to support the claim that there is a connection between better predictions and getting closer to the truth is a good inference. The only riposte left, then, for the determined sceptic is to question the process of induction itself. But neither Laudan nor van Fraasen can make this move without changing their own rules of the game of science and thereby giving up the idea of scientific rationality altogether.

The details of this defence of realism are taken up in what follows, but the important thing to emphasise at this point is that this kind of argument makes sense only if we think of verisimilitude or approximation to the truth as something other than the accumulation of more true than false propositions in our record of scientific progress. Using the concept of verisimilitude as we have developed it we measure the degree to which a scientific research programme gets closer to the truth in terms of the degree of similarity between a model and the real system that it represents. Giere (1988) too has advocated this idea. However, we cannot meaningfully make such a comparison between a theory (as a model or as a chunk of a type-hierarchy) and the world simply by comparing the size of sets of true propositions about the model and what it represents. To be able to do so we would already have to know the truth about the world! So, in order to run these experiments and inductively establish a connection between verisimilitude and a series of theories giving increasingly better predictions, we need a metric that compares objects or entire systems with respect to similarity. We will see that similarity in this context is by no means propositional. The very idea of scientific progress, of getting closer to the truth, is not a matter of numbers of propositions. Progress is to be thought of in metaphysical terms. It is a function of the structure of a type-hierarchy which, in turn, depends on how nature itself is organised into natural kinds.

'Science', as an enterprise, seems to have accumulated a vast stock of reliable knowledge about the natural world. It seems hardly credible that the scientific achievements of the last five hundred years are really just the projections of successive conceptual systems on to an inchoate mass of indeterminate human experiences. How could anyone come to be believe such a thing? Contemporary scepticism is deeply rooted in conceptual relativism. The relativist position depends, we believe, on two main theses: that the content of 'facts' is exhausted by the concepts needed to formulate them; and that no claim to have the truth is secure against possible revision. If the achievements of the scientific community consisted only in piling up statements, the relativists would at least be on a defensible starting point. But 'science' is quite as much a matter of material practices as it is discursive. The scientific community has not only filled libraries with writings, it has also accumulated museums full of specimens of the natural kinds that lie behind its working type-hierarchies, and laboratories full of equipment for manipulating many of those entities in the existence of which sceptics find it so hard to believe. The shift from a propositional to a type-hierarchy account of verisimilitude fits nicely with a shift from an exclusive attention to the discursive practices of science to its material and practical side. 'Science' is realised just as much in experimental techniques as it is in learned articles. This too makes sense only in the framework of the ontosemantics we shall be developing. Perhaps only thus can we explain the neglect of experimental procedures in the traditional philosophy of science.

Finally in this chapter we shall try to lay out clearly how we mean to use the word 'theory' and some other related expressions. We can no longer rely, if we ever could, on an unequivocal common usage among philosophers, scientists and lay folk alike. By 'theory' we will mean any discursive presentation of a community's beliefs, at some definite historical moment, about the causal substructure of some aspects of their world, whether or not this substructure is perceived directly, as a motor mechanic might observe the mechanism that shifts the gears, or indirectly through a model or models, by which a physicist might conceive the content of a theory. By a 'theory-family' we will mean a sequence of theories, resembling one another with respect to the phenomena they are directed towards and their shared or 'common' ontology. We will be using the term 'phenomenon' much as Niels Bohr seems to have meant it. A phenomenon is an observed state of an apparatus/world ensemble as categorised by reference to a locally accepted type-hierarchy. As we shall use the term, a theory is not a model or a set of models (Giere, 1988). Models form the content of theories and sets of models the content of theory-families. Though a theory may have a propositional presentation, we would like to repeat that for us the content of a theory is always to be taken entitatively.

We should emphasise, and shall spell out in detail as we proceed, that by 'model' we shall, unless it is otherwise specified, mean 'iconic model'. Our models, though sometimes rather sketchy or abstract, are entitative. Models, as the term is used in science, are to be understood as instantiating types or kinds.

The way we want to use the word 'law' must also be carefully specified. In the natural sciences laws find expression in general statements, attended with a *ceteris paribus* clause. It would be easy to slip into thinking that the content of a law is the proposition expressed in the law statement. In our move away from a propositional treatment of the problems of the philosophy of science laws too are relocated. A law is to be thought of as an invariant relation among properties, which is expressed propositionally.

We shall be introducing further key terms as we develop our arguments. These will include 'virtual world' as constituted by a model or models in use in a particular episode of theorising, and 'common ontology', the hierarchically ordered system of natural kinds from which a scientific community's virtual worlds are drawn, as it builds, modifies and discards models.

CHAPTER TWO

The Language of Science

1. The structure of the argument

It is important to bear in mind that we are not primarily concerned with the question of how we decide whether an individual belongs to a kind, artifactual, conventional or natural. Rather our project is to give an account of what it means to say that it does. There have been two main trends in attempts to treat our question. According to one point of view, what it is to say that an individual belongs to a kind is to assert that it possesses a certain set of properties, and that it is this set of properties that the kind term designates. The other line is to treat kinds extensionally. On this view an individual belongs to a kind if it is a member of a certain class, and it is that class that the relevant kind term designates. Neither of these proposals is satisfactory. In the course of this chapter we shall show that a natural kind is a set of individuals each of which displays at least some of a certain cluster of properties and that the total set of properties germane to each kind, cluster in the way they do because they somehow reflect the causal substructure of the world. The unique feature of our treatment is the way in which we have substituted a model world serving as a knowledge-representation system for the traditional idea that all knowledge/world relationships must be discussed in terms of a wholly propositional way of representing knowledge. In the model world a type (which represents a natural kind in the real world) is a set of individuals each of which has certain properties which are numerically identical with those in other sets of higher type. Thus an individual 'a' which is in the set 'whale' in the model world is numerically identical with an individual 'b' which is in the set 'mammal', and there are properties of that individual 'a', say 'R', which are numerically identical with properties, say 'S', of the corresponding individual 'b'. In the model world we are not comparing properties of whales with properties of mammals. In saying that whales are mammals we are asserting that some of the properties of whales just *are* properties of mammals.

The terms 'kind' and 'type' have been used in a variety of ways in philosophy. We shall use the word 'kind' for what is on the side of the world, and the word 'type' for what is on the side of representations of the world, as in the above sketch of our position. A natural kind then is something in the world, while a type-hierarchy is a representation of something that is in the world. Each particular in either the real world or the model world has its unique properties. When we speak of a property common to a set of particulars in the real world or the model world, whether it be the members of a natural kind or of a set representing them, we shall mean that there is a qualitative identity between the relevant concrete properties of each particular. Numerical identity of properties obtains between the members of higher and lower sets ordered in a type-hierarchy. These relations exist only in the model world of the knowledge-representation system.

The basic idea behind our point of view is this: in the real world there is just one set of objects, each of which has its own cluster of properties. Instead of attempting to represent our knowledge of this real world primarily in propositions or in terms of sets which are defined only by their members, we propose to represent that knowledge in a model world. However, creating the model or knowledge-representing world on the basis of an ontology that is a mere mirror of the ontology of the real world is inadequate in all sorts of ways. In our treatment the relation between the multiplicity of properties of the one set of entities that constitutes the real world is represented in the model world by splitting the ontology of the model world into a hierarchy of sets of entities, each set distinguished by the properties common to the members, where the multiplicity of properties of an entity in the real world is represented by the multiplicity of sets of ordered pairs of entities each with just one property in the model world. In creating this structure we make use of a basic, unanalysed similarity relation, the qualitative identity of properties. This model world is a system of type-hierarchies. To express our knowledge of the real world we establish two identity mappings, one between the entities which are members of these sets and the other between their properties. Thus each entity in the real world is represented by a set of sets of entities in the model world, one drawn from each set in the type-hierarchy. The model world entity sets are tied together by the sequence of identity mappings with which our knowledge of the property relations of individual real-world things is represented. Similarly the properties of entities in the real world are also represented by an identity mapping, in that the properties of entities in the subtypes in the type-hierarchies are identical with the properties of the entities on to which they are mapped in the supertypes. Of course, this procedure represents what makes a whale a mammal. It does not deal with what it is that makes each whale a whale. We shall address that question when we come to set out our account of natural kinds.

The case for a generally realist interpretation of scientific discourse would be greatly strengthened if we could show that the way that the language of the physical sciences has meaning is fixed, in part, by the way the world is. While acknowledging the place of convention in the development of terminologies we shall argue that the way the language of physical science has meaning cannot be accounted for wholly in terms of arbitrary linguistic conventions. However, the traditional way in which the tie between language and world was thought to be made, through the extensionist treatment of kind terms, is unsatisfactory. Our first task then is to establish a way of understanding kind terms that is naturalistic but free of the objections to extensional analyses. We shall first survey some of the ways that have been proposed to account for the meaning of type concepts. Then we shall look at various accounts of the interrelations of types into structured hierarchies. We shall then be in a position to defend the view that the type-hierarchies that lie behind the way the terminology of a natural science is used by its practitioners are tied in with what is known or believed about the real structures of natural kinds.

Any viable theory of meaning must incorporate the lessons taught by Austin and Wittgenstein: that is, the meaning of an expression is the use that a speaker is understood by his or her interlocutors to be making of it in a particular context. However, the way speakers use words and hearers understand them involves the language community's knowledge and beliefs. We can express such knowledge and belief in the metaphor of a speech community's 'models' or concrete conceptions of their universe and of the nature of its constituents. We think of such things in terms of natural and artificial kinds. We manage our uses of type-words by locating the types with which we represent the kinds of things which we use them to describe on some suitable type-hierarchy and in terms of the internal relations among their parts. The key questions then, for us, are how do kind terms get their meanings, and how are meaningful kind terms related to one another?

2. How kinds are constituted and a type-terminology acquires its meaning

In this section we shall examine critically a number of proposals for treating the problem of how kinds are constituted and how kind terms acquire their meaning. We shall also try to show how the defects which appear in the proposals we examine can be remedied by the theory of type-hierarchies upon which our general treatment of the representation of knowledge about kinds depends.

a. Deficiencies in the view that kinds are the product of judgments of similarity

It is important to distinguish between two main contexts in which use is made of the notion of 'similarity'. We can compare things by noticing similarities and differences between properties. On the basis of such comparisons we often make judgments about similarities and differences between things. It is the latter notion, not the former, that is sometimes used as the basic or unanalysed notion to explain how types and kinds are constituted. The notion of similarity between entities is basic to many accounts of the constitution of kinds and types. However, the relation itself is rarely explicated and is usually treated as a primitive or basic concept too obvious to need explication. This, however, is a grave mistake. Similarity is not the straightforward symmetrical and transitive relation many philosophers and psychologists have assumed it to be. In his well-known study of the features of the similarity relation, Amos Tversky (1977) provides empirical evidence for significant and systematic asymmetries in comparison and production tasks involving similarity. On the basis of this evidence he argues that similarity should not be treated as a symmetrical relation. The statement 'a is like b' is not generally taken to entail 'b is like a'. 'Billboards are like warts' does not entail that warts are like billboards. Furthermore, it follows from the asymmetry of the similarity relation in actual use that it is not transitive either. The direction of the asymmetries appears to be determined in part by the relative importance of the objects compared as well as the attributive direction of a statement of comparison.

Similarity is not a constant and stable relation between two entities, but varies widely depending on context. For example, judgments of similarity between the colours white and grey is different in different contexts. Medin and Shoben (1988) found that white hair and grey hair were judged to be more similar than grey hair and black hair, but that the similarity judgment reverses in the context of clouds. White clouds and grey clouds were judged as less similar than grey clouds and black clouds. Medin and Shoben also showed that a property or feature equally true (or false) of two objects may be more central to the concept of the one than of the other. For example, it was found that it is more important that boomerangs be curved than bananas. A match between boomerangs and bananas in this respect is neither here nor there. Some matching features between two objects will be more important than others in making judgments of similarity.

Medin (1989) characterises some of the assumptions which are frequently made in the way people make judgments of similarity:

(1) Similarity between two things increases as a function of the number of features or properties they share and decreases as a function of mismatching or distinctive features.
(2) These features can be treated as independent and additive.
(3) The features determining similarity are all at roughly the same level of abstraction.

However, we have seen that similarity cannot be characterised in terms of the number of matches between independent features. Rather all the evidence points to the fact that it is our knowledge about the objects and how they interrelate that determines what features count as relevant in judgments of similarity in different situations. The reason why it is more important for judgments of similarity that boomerangs be curved than bananas is that the curvature is responsible for a boomerang's distinctive flight, whereas bananas are only curved as an accident of growth. Bananas would still have all their important properties even if they were straight. Our experience tells us that grey and white hair colours usually indicate greater age for humans and animals, whereas black hair usually does not. However, grey and black clouds both indicate stormy weather, where white clouds do not. Our knowledge of how objects behave when thrown, of age-related physiological changes and of weather conditions all contribute to the relative salience of the features of objects of comparison. In other words, similarity between things is dynamically determined. It is based upon our beliefs about and models of the world. According to Medin (1989: 1474), 'It is perhaps only a modest exaggeration to say that similarity gets at the shadow rather than the substance of concepts. Something is needed to give concepts life, coherence, and meaning. Although many philosophers of science have argued that observations are necessarily theory-laden only recently have researchers begun to stress that the organisation of concepts is knowledge-based and driven by theories of the world.' Thus the question arises: do things belong in the same category because they have common features or do their common features become 'visible' because they are put in the same category? The weakness of feature matching as the basis for those judgments of similarity upon which the collection of similar things into common kinds is based leads us towards the latter alternative.

The above discussion invites one to view categorisation as attribute matching under a relevance or salience constraint. However, most categories are not a simple sum of independent features. Structuring relations are needed to make, for example, a bunch of bird features into a bird. The features alone do not make a bird, they interact in specified ways to create a coherent whole. For instance, the tendency to build nests in trees is related to having wings and laying eggs, and having feathers and hollow bones is related to the ability to fly. Keil (1979, 1981) has pointed out that many commonplace categories such as 'robin' and 'squirrel' collect up diverse entities that share many important properties that almost never show up in people's listings of attributes for a category. For example, has a heart, breathes, sleeps, is an organism, is an object with boundaries, is a physical object, is a thing, can be thought about, and so on. The number of properties which any two things might have in common could be infinite. Murphy and Medin (1985) point out that plums and lawnmowers both weigh less than 1,000 kg, both are found on earth, both are found in our solar system, both cannot hear well, both have an odour, both are not worn by elephants, both are used by people, both can be dropped, and so on. Yet in most contexts these matching features would not be used by anyone to put instances of these types into the same category.

Without constraints on what is to count as a relevant feature for matching, any two things could be said to be similar or dissimilar to any degree. In these circumstances judgments of similarity and dissimilarity are arbitrary. What is more, there are many properties which are defined only relative to some arbitrary standard. For instance, an eagle is a large bird, but is a much smaller animal than a small elephant. Features like large, small, big, heavy, tall, thin, fat, old, young, hairy, bald, etc., are all highly dependent upon the standards for each domain. Even worse, we have the same problem for individual features. All the members sharing a particular feature, say having wings, are related to other members only by various groupings of similarities. The wings of an eagle vary greatly from the wings of a chicken, a bat or penguin. What makes these diverse particular instances of wings part of the same general feature? They are not all used for flying, some of the wings have feathers while others do not. They all seem to have criss-crossing and over-lapping qualitative similarities, but is this enough to delineate the feature? As we will see in the next section, using partial shared similarity as the sole criterion for category (or feature) membership leads to groupings where some members may not have any features at all in common. If this is the case, how are similarity judgments made at all, and how do the various instances relate to a prototype? We will return to these questions in the next section, after we consider the Wittgensteinian notion of family resemblances.

b. Limitations to the idea of family resemblance between entities as constitutive of kinds

Wittgenstein in his later work (1953), offered a wide range of arguments against the view that each word had a unitary, essential and hence permanent core of meaning. The doctrine of essential meanings obscured the actual workings of language, and led directly to the adoption of false linguistic models, engendering intractable philosophical problems. According to Wittgenstein, language is used as an integral part of human activity and culture. Social customs, human action and institutions, clustered into 'forms of life', are constituted by and constitute the conventions of language use. 'To imagine a language is to imagine a form of life.' Thus, our language forms and restricts our lives and, in turn, is formed and restricted by them. Uses are not fixed by reference to dictionaries, nor to lists of necessary properties nor by the rules of logic which capture only certain static fragments of the way language functions in life. Wittgenstein uses the concept of a language game to emphasise that linguistic responses can be understood only as a part of complex human activities: 'Here the term "language-game" is meant to bring into prominence the fact that the speaking of language is part of an activity, or of a form of life.'

Wittgenstein's socio-anthropological approach to language treats meaning as activity-dependent, where the necessary and sufficient conditions for the use of an expression must also include a description of the activity with which it is involved and the societal commitments which accompany its use.

Wittgenstein particularly rejects the view that words can have clear-cut boundaries of use. He claims that we cannot explain the whole of the use of many very common words by reference to some common essence in everything comprehended under the *word* nor by reference to some list of necessary and sufficient conditions for the correct application of the word. For example, consider the word 'dog', and its myriad of uses: to talk about a pet, a food ('hot dog'), a despicable person ('dirty dog'), fire irons ('fire dogs'), a fortunate person ('lucky dog'), a degree of tiredness ('dog tired'), feet ('my dogs'), a kind of day ('dog days'), a way to be persistent ('dogged his footsteps'), an ugly person ('a real dog'), a way to show off ('putting on dog'), and so on. Instead of assuming there must be a common essence, if we actually examine instances of the uses of a given lexical item we find 'a complicated network of similarities overlapping and crisscrossing: sometimes overall similarities, sometimes similarities of detail' (Wittgenstein, 1953: 66). Thus, according to Wittgenstein, what we perceive as similar among the members of all the uses of a *word* is a family resemblance among them. Thus there are no clear boundaries delineating what can or cannot be considered to fall under a concept or a word; one word can map to (comprehend) many concepts, and one concept may be exemplified by the uses of many words. Bambrough (1961) gives an account of what it means for concepts to comprehend an array of applications to a number of objects that share only a 'family resemblance':

> We may classify a set of objects by reference to the presence or absence of features ABCDE. It may well happen that five objects edcba are such that each of them has four of these properties and lacks the fifth, and that the missing feature is different in each of the five cases. A sample diagram will illustrate this situation: (Bambrough, 1961: 112)

a	e	d	c	b
ABCD	ABCE	ABDE	ACDE	BCDE

Although there are Wittgenstein scholars who do not feel that Bambrough's example captures the true extent of Wittgenstein's idea, we have used it here because it gives us a clear account of how family resemblance can work. The above example demonstrates how several different things may sufficiently resemble each other so that they are classified under the same general concept, and yet not have a single feature in common. Furthermore, Bambrough points out, actual features may not fit neatly into divisions as tidy as the ABCDE above. The instances of the feature A, for example, may also be family-resemblant in nature. He concludes that it is possible to have a concept where no two members have any feature in common and yet all the members still share a family resemblance.

Will this account do for the solution to our problem? According to the family resemblance theory of the way words comprehend groups of entities there need be no central core or essence which can be used to explain the range of a word's uses. Wittgenstein's major point is that if we look for features in common among the objects picked out by a word we cannot always expect to find one. So talking of a central core of common features is very like returning to a list of necessary and sufficient conditions for word meaning. Family resemblance theory holds that there is democracy among the objects picked out by many common words. No one is more central than another in fixing what the word *really* means. Nor are the uses of words independent of context.

However, Wittgenstein would not have wanted to deny that there are some uses of a word which depend on recognition of a core of properties common to the objects picked out by it. There may be no common core to the objects comprehended by the word 'game', but there certainly is to those comprehended by the word 'soccer'. He would have denied that the very same core will account for *all* the ways a common word is or could be used. In Wittgenstein's 'city of language' the modern suburbs have straight streets and a rectangular layout. The use of scientific and technical terminologies may well be based on sets of common properties. It is Waismann's (1968) notion of 'open texture' that applies to the terms of a scientific discourse, not so much Wittgenstein's 'family resemblance'. According to Waismann the structure of a scientific terminology is such that there is always an open question as to how our ways of describing a new instance are to be fitted into an existing type-hierarchy. No hierarchy is so complete that it is predetermined how we should use it to deal with marginal cases. This is a point which we shall be emphasising throughout this book. Type-hierarchies are sensitive to the state of our empirical knowledge and the articulations of our theoretical concepts.

c. Weaknesses in the idea that kinds are constituted by reference to a prototype and a core

What is the nature of this centre around which the field of family resemblant entities cluster? One recently popular theory based on empirical studies of how people classify groups of disparate objects depends on the idea of a prototype. This raises several questions. How do we come to 'have' prototypes? Does the bird prototype represent some kind of averaging of features across all birds? Prototypes are not like that. When the beanbag chair was invented our prototype chair did not change from, say, a wooden ladder back to something somewhat less rigid. A prototype 'stands for' a kind or type but does not represent the average member. In the case of many common classes it is hard to see what would it mean to create a bird-prototype by taking an 'average' of a penguin, a hummingbird, a robin and an albatross.

However, the theory that kinds are thought about through the uses of prototypes implies that the only information necessary for common meaning for a category term like 'bird' is that concerning the central exemplar. A prototype representation cannot convey information concerning category size, the variability of examples or information concerning correlations of attributes. However, people are sensitive to all these aspects of kinds (Medin 1989: 1472). Most people adhere to the belief that small birds are much more likely to sing than large birds. This intuition cannot be obtained from a single summary prototype for birds.

If the prototype is not a result of distilling our accumulated experiences of instances of that kind, then it seems that a prototype is picking out something more than a best example. It seems that prototypical is not just *typical*, but something more. Keil notes:

> An unpacking of why prototypical features 'play a role in meanings of words' whereas typical features do not may illustrate some fundamental limitations of the whole approach of prototype semantics that Coleman and Kay so warmly embrace in their paper. In particular, the 'prototypical features' may be central to meaning just because they *are* centrally involved in other more explanatory sets of relations. (Keil, 1989: 29)

Furthermore if the prototype does occupy a central position in such discursive practices as explanation then we must already know something about the concept it is to exemplify, or we could not construct it. So it cannot serve to explicate the concept itself. There is another way to bring out this circularity. The real problem cases for deciding what concept an object falls under occur when we have an object that appears not to resemble any prototype: for example, a plastic lump in the middle of a room. We may later decide that this object is an instance of a new type of furniture, but such a decision may have nothing to do with any similarity it may have to one of a set of furniture prototypes. It is true that the plastic lump can serve as an additional paradigm of furniture for other things to cluster about; yet such a role comes *after* it is determined that what we have is a furniture piece. The point is that using prototypes to determine whether or not an object falls under a concept puts the cart before the horse. The similarities between the inherent properties of things do not determine whether they fall under the same concept. Rather, that they fall under the same concept tells us that we must look for similarities between them.

However, E.E. Smith claims that 'The proposal that an ordinary concept includes only a prototype turns out to be too simple. A more defensible claim is that an ordinary concept contains two components – a prototype and a core. The prototype contains properties that are useful for a "quick and dirty" categorisation of objects, where such properties tend to be perceptually salient and easy to compute, though not very diagnostic of concept membership. In contrast, the properties that comprise the core are more diagnostic of concept membership but tend to be relatively hidden and less accessible for rapid categorisation' (Smith, 1989: 509).

Ignoring the category muddles in this paragraph exemplified in the strange notion of 'concept membership', we can say that while the concept 'Bird' has sub-concepts referring to the properties listed for its prototype, its core might include other sub-concepts, such as 'bird-genes' or 'bird parentage'. With this addition we seem to have come back to a familiar and traditional account of kind terms, namely that of nominal and real essences. The prototype seems to function like the nominal essence, while the core sounds suspiciously like real essence.

Although there do seem to be some items that are more prototypical than others falling under the same concept, and even though most people can reliably rank members as being more or less prototypical, it does not follow that prototypes can be used to *explain* why our concepts are structured the way they are. Nor do prototypes provide a mechanism for classifying new instances under this or that type or kind.

The upshot of this critical survey suggests that a combination of family resemblance as the general account of type formation with refinements and distinctions for special classes of words is likely to serve us well (Rundle, 1990). But developing these refinements and distinctions will bring out the extent to which type formation is dependent on our theories of how the world is.

3. How types are interrelated in hierarchies

We remind the reader that by 'types' we mean representations of kinds. Types are on the side of the mind, kinds on the side of the world. One of the most difficult and persistent problems for semantic network theory has been to explicate the relationship between the nodes of the network and the links between them. This problem arises in particular for the kind of network known as a generalisation hierarchy, the very form of hierarchy which our type-hierarchies take. Generalisation hierarchies arrange types or categories with highly general ones like THING or ENTITY at the top of the hierarchy to more specific types like TABLE or CAT on lower levels. These hierarchies seem to capture our common-sense notions of the ordering of representations of kinds of things, and for this reason, they have been widely used in all sorts of knowledge representation systems.

Early hierarchy schemes were notorious for their intuitive and *ad hoc* use of '*isa*' links between types: that is, for setting up links like 'A tiger *is a* feline quadruped'. Even contemporary researchers struggle with the problem of formulating a precise account of the semantics of this relation. Many different characterisations have been given for the linkages between nodes in the hierarchy. These include class membership, sets of intensions, genus-species and entailment. We will see below that all of these characterisations run into serious difficulties. Sowa discusses the problem as follows:

> There is no universally accepted terminology for the type-hierarchy. The symbol < between a more specialised type and a more general type may be read *is a subtype of, is a subset of, is a subsort of, is a kind of, is a flavour of,* or simply *isa.* Unfortunately there are objections to all of these terms. (Sowa 1987: 1016)

In this chapter we want to revive the old distinction between determinables and determinates. This relation is different from any of the above, and we believe it can shed some light on the interpretation of the nodes and links in a generalisation hierarchy. However, before we show how the determinable-determinate relation can resolve many of the problems posed by the *'isa'* relation, we will show why some of the other candidates for the link relation of a semantic hierarchy run into trouble.

a. Difficulties with the theory that type-hierarchies are formed by class inclusion

One of the most widely used interpretations of semantic hierarchies is as an ordering of classes. On this view, the nodes represent classes of things in the world and the links the relation of class inclusion. Thus the node which represents DOG really denotes the class of all dogs in the world, and the node representing ANIMAL is the class of all animals, of which DOG is a subclass. The partial ordering on the hierarchy will then just be the relation of class inclusion, which is asymmetrical and transitive. Inheritance corresponds to the transitivity of class inclusion: if dogs are mammals and if mammals nurse their young, then dogs nurse their young.

On the surface, this sounds like a perfectly acceptable account of how we order our concepts of kinds of things. However, it quickly runs into trouble. Adopting the standard terminology we shall say that the class of things that a term picks out in the world is the *extension* of that term. To talk of these classes as determining our concepts is to define concepts *extensionally*. However, the problem with defining concepts extensionally is that we often have *different* concepts which pick out the *same* class of things in the world. The traditional example of co-extensive classes is the class of creatures with hearts and the class of creatures with lungs. These classes are picked out with the help of two different concepts but they pick out the same set of things in the world. That is, everything which has a heart also happens to have a lung. If our concepts are based on the structure of classes in the world to begin with, how can we account for the fact that we have two different concepts for the very same class of things? We cannot explain this with class inclusion alone. If class inclusion is used to explicate the structure of the nodes of a hierarchy of type concepts, then the concept of having a heart and that of having a lung will *have to* be the same concept.

This would lead to disastrous results for the structure of our semantic hierarchy. For example, imagine a world where colour and shape were co-extensive, that is, where the class of all things with shape is coextensive with the class of all things which are coloured.

COLOUR = SHAPE

GREEN BLUE RED ROUND SQUARE CIRCLE

Then, by class inclusion, RED would be not only a colour but also a shape, and SQUARE would be both a shape and a colour. Furthermore, the members of the subclasses of shape would inherit all the properties we normally ascribe to colour and the subtypes of colour would inherit all the properties for shapes.

Clearly, this is not how we ordinarily structure our concepts. 'Red' is *not* a shape concept nor 'square' a colour concept. What is missing in this analysis is a way of defining the notions of 'colour' and 'shape' independently of the things which happen to be coloured or shaped. The contingencies of class membership alone do not seem to be sufficient to account for how our concepts are ordered.

b. Problems with the theory that type-hierarchies are expressible in terms of a common extension and intension

Philosophers have introduced various distinctions to account for the discrepancy between the way we structure our concepts or language and the structure of classes of things in the world. Frege (1892) originated the distinction between the *sense* of a concept and its *referent*. He was concerned with the problem of accounting for the existence of informative identity statements. How is it that a statement like 'the morning star "is" the evening star' is informative while a statement like 'the morning star "is" the morning star' is not. Since both the terms 'morning star' and 'evening star' refer to the same thing in the world, namely Venus, how can one be informative while the other is not? Frege's answer is that while the *referent* of the morning star and evening star is the same, the *senses* of the two are not. Thus the concepts of the morning star and evening star differ in their cognitive content. One means 'the brightest star in the morning' and the other means 'the brightest star in the evening'. In this way, we could know both concepts and still learn something new by being told that they refer to the same thing.

Woods (1975) discusses the need for a *semantics* of semantic networks, and recommends incorporating these distinctions:

> To begin, I would like to raise the distinction between intension and extension, a distinction that has been variously referred to as the difference between sense and reference, meaning and denotation and various other pairs of terms.

Woods then proposes that semantic networks be modelled on intensions of concepts rather than on extensional sets of entities. He feels however, that such a change will require a major reinterpretation of the semantics of semantic networks. Many have followed Woods' recommendation, and try to treat the nodes in semantic hierarchies intensionally. In this way, types do not represent classes of entities but are intensions. The partial ordering on the network is still that of class inclusion, though 'inclusion' will be understood quite differently. Thus, the type DOG will correspond to our *sense* of dog but it will still be a subtype of the type which corresponds to our *sense* of MAMMAL. The question is, does this reinterpretation of the meaning of the nodes avoid the problems we encountered earlier with class inclusion?

Unfortunately, there are still problems with this interpretation of a semantic net; for how are we to interpret the relation between intensions? The fact is that if we use class inclusion to order the nodes of the hierarchy, then the nodes still have to denote classes. For every intension there is a corresponding extension. Thus, although we have a sense or meaning for the concept 'dog', it also will have an extension, which is all the actual (and possible) dogs. By introducing the notion of a class intension, we are able to distinguish two classes in our intensional network by virtue of their members having different defining attributes, for example,that of *having a heart* and that of *having a lung*. However, a class is constituted by its members, and if everything in the world which has a heart also has a lung and *vice versa*, then the classes corresponding to the two intensions in the hierarchy will have to be constituted by the same members. Let us return to the world where something has colour if and only if it has shape. Even though these classes are co-extensive, we still have different intensions of the class terms 'colour' and 'shape', because they represent different attributes of an object. But, if the relation between these intensions is class inclusion, then what we really have are two classes whose members are identical and, as a result, whose subtypes have multiple parents. Thus, as it was for extensions and class inclusion, with intensions, the subtype RED is not only a subtype of COLOUR but also of SHAPE.

It is easy to see why so many exponents of artificial intelligence have used class membership to order their hierarchies: it is a powerful and well-defined system. However it is inadequate to the task of representing the relation between the nodes of a hierarchy in a way which naturally motivates the actual arrangements of subtypes and supertypes that we find in hierarchical systems in use in science and elsewhere. To achieve this we shall make use of the distinction between determinables and their determinates.

c. Hierarchical organisation based on the relation of determinate to determinable

The determinate-determinable distinction seems to explicate many of our intuitions about what it means for one type to fall under another. Like the subtype-supertype relation, it is often seen as one of specificity. The determin*ate* (e.g. RED) is more *specific* than the determin*able* (e.g. COLOUR). In other words, if something is red it is coloured but if it is coloured it is not necessarily red. The problem here is that specificity alone is not enough to explicate the relation. Terms that stand solely in the relation of lesser specificity to greater do not always capture the relation of subtype to supertype nor that of determinate to determinable. For example, as Searle (1959) points out, RED is more specific than RED OR ANGRY but it is not a determinate of RED OR ANGRY in the same way as it is a determinate of COLOUR.

The terminology for determinates and determinables came into existence in scholastic philosophy but the modern use of these terms began with Johnson (1921). More recently it has been revived by Prior (1949), Korner (1959), Armstrong (1978), Fales (1982), Searle (1959) and Hautamaki (1986). Johnson explicates the determinable-determinate relation as based on the logical division of classes into subclasses. However, the relation is not class inclusion nor is it to be confused with the traditional division of classes into *genus* and species. It was developed by scholastic philosophers in response to problems with Aristotle's method. Aristotle held that a species could be defined by the intersection of its *genus* and its *differentia*. Thus, the class or species of 'man' is included within the class of its *genus*, 'animal', but marked off from other classes within the *genus* by the *differentia* of rationality.

The point here is that a species is characterised by the intersection of two logically independent properties: the *differentia* and the *genus*. But there is no such device for characterising the determinable-determinate relation. A determinate is not an intersection of its determinable and any other class that is logically independent of that specific determinate. (The *differentiae* are considered logically independent in that alone, they cannot constitute the *genus*.)

For example, it was realised that RED could not be characterised by the intersection of COLOUR and anything (except RED or something synonymous with it). Yet 'red' is a specific instance of 'colour'. Both the genus-species and the determinate-determinable relations are relations of the less specific to the more specific. But in the genus-species relation, specification is provided by some property logically independent of the *genus*, while the determinate-determinable relation cannot be specified by adding additional independent properties to the determinable.

There are some other interesting features about this distinction. First, the determinates under the same determinable are considered to be *incompatible*. For example, something cannot be both red and green *at the same point* on an object at the same time; red and green are determinates of the same determinable and, hence, are incompatible. However, according to Johnson, determinates under a determinable are *comparable*. In fact, Johnson sees the determinates as assuming a certain serial order, where, for example, the difference between red and orange is less than that between red and yellow.

Secondly, the determinates under a given determinable must completely exhaust all aspects of it. Thus, all the determinates under the determinable 'colour' will be collectively exhaustive of 'colour'. Searle talks about determinates competing for position within the area covered by the determinable, competing, that is, for a part of the determinable to specify.

Thirdly, the division of a determinable into the set of determinates is based on some principle of *'fundamentum divisionis'*. In many cases, a class of things is divided according to colour, size or some other aspect with which they can be compared. This aspect constitutes the *fundamentum divisionis*. However, exactly what this principle of fundamental division is or how it works, Johnson does not say.

Searle's formulation attempts to clarify the intuitive notion of specificity by defining five conditions for deciding when any two terms stand in the determinate-determinable relation to each other. He gives a formal characterisation of each of his criteria but we can explain them informally.

The first criterion is that of *specificity*, which was mentioned above. It states that a determinate entails its determinable but the determinable does not entail its determinate. Thus, a determinate must be a *specifier* of its determinable.

The second condition is that the relation is not that of genus-species: there is no third logically independent property (that is, no *differentia*) such that when it is combined with the determinable it constitutes the determinate. For example, we cannot get the colour red by combining another property – a *differentia* – with colour. In other words, for a term A to be a determinate of a term B, A must be an *undifferentiated specifier* of its determinable B.

The third criterion is for the non-conjunctive nature of the determinates. Whatever entails the determinable cannot be broken up into parts where one of the conjuncts does all the work of specifying the determinable. The motivation for this criterion is that, so far, the first two criteria have not been able to rule out examples such as 'red rose' as determinates of colour. Being non-conjunctive entails being *undifferentiated*, so we now have as a necessary condition of A's being a determinate of B that A is a *non-conjunctive specifier* of B.

The fourth requirement is meant to rule out the difficulty that a more specific expression like 'red' can be considered as a determinate of the more general determinable of the form 'red or angry'. This condition states that determinates specify their determinables in such a way that the determinable and determinate are *logically related* to each other (and to other determinables). By 'logically related to each other' Searle means that for any two terms, either entails the other or either entails the negation of the other. Searle (1959: 148) explains it this way:

> Genuine determinates under a determinable compete with each other for position within the same area, they are, as it were, in the same line of business, and for this reason they will stand in certain logical relations to each other.

Thus, for any two terms A and B, A is a determinate of B if and only if A is a non-conjunctive specifier of B, and A is logically related to all other non-conjunctive specifiers of B.

Searle's fifth condition is a criterion for same level determinates. 'Two terms A and B are *same-level determinates* of C if and only if they are both determinates of C and neither is a specifier of the other.' Thus, red, blue and green are all *same-level determinates*. However, a term like scarlet, even though it is a specifier of colour, cannot be on the same level as red, blue and green, since it is also a specifier of red.

Searle also discusses the notion of an *absolute* determinable that all lower-order determinables fall under. For example, scarlet is a determinate of red but both are determinates of the absolute determinable colour. He explains this notion as follows:

> We may think of colour terminology as providing us with a hierarchy of terms, many of which will stand in the determinable relation to each other as the specification of shades progresses from the less precise to the more precise. But at the top of the hierarchy stands the term 'colour', which we may describe as an absolute determinable of all the other members of the hierarchy, including such lower-order determinables as 'red' and their determinates, such as 'scarlet'. (Searle, 1959: 149)

Here we see a hierarchical ordering emerge from this distinction, as well as the idea of absolute determinables, which many philosophers have seen as a form of generic universals. With the introduction of the idea of an absolute determinable, we must now rephrase the previous point: determinates of the same determinable are incompatible *unless* one of the determinates is a lower-order determinable of the other. Finally, determinates *presuppose* their absolute determinables; for an object to have the determinate, say scarlet, predicated of it, it must also have colour.

Hautamaki (1986) has pointed out a major weakness of Searle's account, namely that all of these conditions are defined in terms of his unanalysed concept of 'entailment'. The relation of determinate and determinable is primarily one of specificity, and Searle's definition is in terms of the determinate *entailing* the determinable but not vice versa. The logical relation between the determinates of a given determinable is also given in terms of entailment: for any two determinates each entails either the other or the negation of the other. Although Searle doesn't say exactly what this 'entailment' is based on, he seems aware of this shortcoming:

> The weakness of this approach on the other hand lies in the inappropriateness of attacking certain areas of ordinary language with such crude weapons as entailment, necessary and sufficient conditions, etc., and the consequent air of unreality surrounding any such approach. Part of Wittgenstein's point in his discussion of family resemblance is simply to cast doubt on any *general* philosophical method of this sort, for not all terms admit of clear-cut analysis of the required kind. We cannot, e.g., say exactly what terms entail or are entailed by 'game'. The criterion then must be taken as an ideal model and not a description of the way language actually works. (Searle, 1959: 150-1)

However, this will not do. We need to say precisely what the link is between determinables and determinates, in what way one entails the other, and what the 'logical relation' is between determinates of the same determinable.

There is another more serious problem with using entailment to explicate the relation between determinables and determinates. It is the same problem that confronted the above rival analyses: if two concepts are coextensive, they can be uniformly substituted in any entailment relation. Thus, by using entailment as a primitive in explicating the determinate-determinable relation, Searle has reintroduced all the problems of co-extensive classes. Once more, in a world where colour and shape pick out the same class of objects, then if being red entails having colour, being red will also entail having shape. Thus, like classes and class inclusion, intensions and class inclusion, entailment is too weak a relation to capture the structure of our concepts.

d. Type-hierarchies ordered by the inheritance of second-order properties under the relation of determinate to determinable

To complete our analysis we shall make use of an important insight from the theory of semantic networks. Semantic networks share a common notation consisting of *nodes* (drawn as dots, circles, or boxes) and *arcs* (or *links*, drawn as arrows) connecting the nodes. Both nodes and links can have labels indicating what they represent. Nodes usually represent *objects, concepts* or *situations* while the links represent the *relations* between them. However, this general outline is often all that is common between various network representations. The type-hierarchy, with which we are working, is a particular kind of semantic network, including complex networks of types or concepts which are organised according to levels of *generality*, or, alternatively *specificity*, where the concepts get more abstract as one moves up the hierarchy and more concrete as one moves down. The nodes at the lowest levels of the hierarchy denote specific individuals or *Tokens*, while nodes at the higher levels denote categories of individuals or *Types*. We need to be careful to maintain the distinction between a type or concept and an instance of that type. Many networks use an *instance-of* link to distinguish between types and individuals. Thus, networks use *isa* links between types and *instance-of* links to connect a particular instance to the type it is an instance of. Sometimes *ako* (*a-kind-of*) links are used between types instead of the *isa* kind. Semantic nets are reflections of natural kinds.

Semantic networks which have types organised according to levels of generality also support a very important property, that of *inheritance*. In a hierarchically structured semantic net the properties and relations of any given type can be *inherited* by all of its subtypes. For example, if we know that canaries are subtypes of birds, and our friend Bob is a canary, then we can conclude that Bob is also a bird, and that he inherits the properties that birds possess.

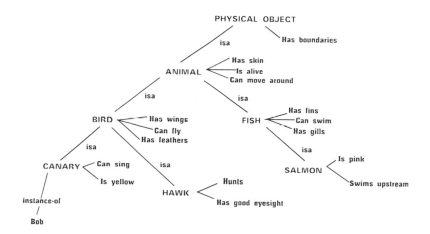

Figure 2.1. An animal type-hierarchy

The hierarchy makes it easy to deduce these facts by a form of *modus ponens*: Bob is a canary, canaries are birds, therefore, Bob is a bird. This is called *an inheritance hierarchy*, or sometimes an *isa*-hierarchy. In this kind of structure many of Bob's properties, such as 'has wings', do not have to be represented explicitly at the node for Bob. That they belong to Bob is implicit in the structure and ordering of the hierarchy. Thus, in order to determine if Bob has a certain property, just trace up the *isa*-hierarchy and assume that any of the meta-properties asserted about higher nodes can be considered assertions about lower nodes as well. The ease with which such deductions can be made has made this representation scheme very popular, especially where the knowledge to be represented is based on a very complicated taxonomy.

Shastri (1988) describes inheritance as follows:

Inheritance is the form of reasoning that leads an agent to infer properties of a concept based on the properties of its ancestors. For example, if the agent knows that 'birds fly', then given that 'Tweety is a bird' he may infer that 'Tweety flies'. This kind of reasoning, often referred to as default reasoning, is commonplace and one can even argue that it is the quintessence of common-sense reasoning.

We shall see that the notion of inheritance is a powerful one that satisfies our commonsense intuitions about the ordering of concepts and the links between them. It is also worth remarking that it is an interpretation of the Aristotelian AII syllogism!

We saw earlier that when using class inclusion as the link between the nodes of a semantic hierarchy, the inheritance relation is accounted for in terms of the transitivity of class inclusion: if dogs are a subset of mammals, and if mammals nurse their young, then dogs nurse their young. Now that we are no longer using class inclusion, the inheritance relation must be examined to see if it can be used to explicate the determinate-determinable distinction. 'Inheritance' states that for all P, if P is a property of a determinable A, then P is also a property of each of A's determinates. For example, if we characterise colour in terms of hue, intensity and saturation then we characterise red, yellow, blue etc., also in these terms. These are meta- or second-order properties because they are properties of a property; in this case, hue, intensity, etc., are properties of the property red.

Thus what collects the determinates under a determinable is the fact that they are all are capable of inheriting meta-properties from that determinable. Note that on this account, colour itself is not a second-order property, and any object which is red will also have the first-order property of colour attributed to it.

Inheritance gives us a way, then, to non-arbitrarily structure hierarchies: according to whether or not the subtypes or determinables can take on the meta-properties of the supertype or determinate parents. The notion of inheritance is also able to help explicate Searle's notion of the logical relation between determinates under the same determinable. They are all 'in the same business' because they all inherit a set of meta-properties from their determinable.

Thus inheritance has to be part of the defining conditions for the determinate-determinable relation. The inheritance of properties by the subtype from the supertype is not something that *follows* from the relation; it is a *defining characteristic* of what it means to be a determinate of a determinable. Thus, we can state a sixth condition for Searle's determinate-determinable relation, namely that, for any two terms A and B, if A is a determinate of B then for any property P, if P is a second-order property of B then P is a second-order property of A.

So far we have investigated the relationship between the determinable and its determinates, and we have seen that it is one of specificity, that determinates somehow carve up the area covered by the determinable and that inheritance is involved. However, we have yet to say exactly what this relationship is or to account for how inheritance occurs. We have seen that Searle's notion of logical entailment is just as problematic as any attempt to use class inclusion. We shall offer our own account in terms of *identity* functions.

4. Type-hierarchies and natural kinds

We now turn to applying these insights to the question of what the type-hierarchies that we find in the natural sciences are about. We contend that the theories of the natural sciences are built upon hierarchies of natural kinds. What is a natural kind? Boyd characterises a natural kind this way:

> [It is] defined by a set or cluster of properties whose membership is determined by the causal structure of the world. (1991: 129)

But we have seen that the attempt to treat kinds wholly in terms of the properties which members display is inadequate. For us a kind is to be defined as follows:

> A natural kind is a set of entities which have a certain cluster of properties in common, that cluster being fixed by the natural laws appropriate to the case.

Natural kinds form the basis of our inductions to the extent that they 'cut the world at its joints'. The point is that whether we are right about which kinds are natural kinds is an empirical question and open to modification in the light of future revision of our theories and laws about the world, and of the results of empirical investigations. It is this point that has been made so fruitfully by Boyd (1991) and Putnam (1983). The same point was also emphasised in the attempt by Harré and Madden (1977) to revitalise the distinction between real and nominal essences.

In this paragraph one of the central ideas of what has been called 'the new theory of reference' appears: the idea that the extension of certain kinds of terms, natural kind words meaning names for such things as natural substances, species, and physical magnitudes) are not fixed by a set of 'criteria' laid down in advance, but are, in part, *fixed by the world*. There are *objective laws* obeyed by multiple sclerosis, by gold, by horses, by electricity; and what is rational to include in the classes of entities constitutive of these kinds will depend on what those laws turn out to be.

It is because we do not know these laws precisely that we have to leave the extension of these classes somewhat open, rather than fixing it exactly by making our kind terms synonymous with sets of necessary and sufficient conditions. Two systems are of the same natural kind to the extent that they obey the same unique set of laws. Of course, this notion of natural kinds entails that there is a unique set of laws for each natural kind. One is reminded of the proverb: If it walks like a duck, quacks like a duck, flies like a duck, ... , it's a duck.

Not only do we subscribe to the doctrine of natural kinds, we also claim that they are ordered along the lines of the determinate-determinable relationship. Combining this with the fact that clusters of laws determine the identity of a natural kind, we must add new information to our type-hierarchy representation of theories: at each node of the hierarchy there is a corresponding set of laws governing the behaviour of the system represented by that particular type. This idea is implicit in the general point of view favouring the primacy of non-propositional knowledge representation with which we began this chapter.

In order to illustrate this point, let us consider various examples of systems in nature that oscillate harmonically. It should be clear that while these systems are distinct in some ways, they are similar in others. In each case, however, there is a unique law governing the period of each system. For example, each simple pendulum is a harmonic system that obeys some of the same laws as do compound pendulums and even the planets. In Figure 2.2 we can see that there is family resemblance between the laws governing each system's period of oscillation.

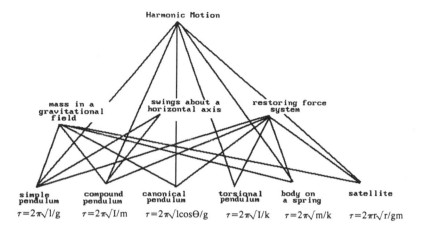

Figure 2.2. A hierarchy of oscillator types

What the above figure illustrates is that each subtype inherits a different combination of supertype laws, yielding a unique law of the system. In the above case, the colour of the system is not a factor determining its location in the natural order, simply because colour does not appear among the terms in any of the above formulae for the period of oscillation of any of the harmonic systems. Sometimes, however, subtypes only have one parent. In this situation each subtype is unique in that the set of laws for each system is a boundary condition of the more general law(s) of the supertype.

The set of laws for each subtype is a special case of the law(s) of combination of the properties of the supertype class. The scope of the law(s) and how they are combined determines which supertypes are to be acknowledged. (Below, we will present an imaginary example of combining +/– particles illustrating this point, a situation very similar to grand unified theories.)

We cannot overemphasise that the set of laws characteristic of each physical system depends on *internal* relationships among its parts. Clearly, a mere aggregate composed of an inelastic string, a mass point and a frictionless ball-bearing do not comprise a simple pendulum. They must be assembled in just the right way. This can be said of any type of system. This information must be located at each node in that type-hierarchy which represents a particular group of natural kinds.

As Putnam has pointed out, the discovery of new laws often forces us to renegotiate the ordering of a type-hierarchy representing certain natural kinds. Kinetic theory reclassified heat as energy while the laws of the special theory of relativity moved rest mass under the supertype, energy, when they replaced the laws of Newtonian mechanics. This feature of the development of the physical sciences is ubiquitous. It shows how the ordering of types in the model world to represent kinds in the real world is always open to revision by reference to empirical considerations, though, as in these examples, the empirical aspect bears rather indirectly through the radical revisions that new discoveries require in the relevant theories.

Critics of the use of the concept of 'natural kind' in the philosophy of science insist that the idea that it is possible to carve nature 'at its joints' is a myth, that the way in which kind terms are used in a taxonomy is entirely a matter of convention. It is not influenced by empirical considerations. This is a tempting position to take in the light of the many ways that nature can be divided into kinds for all sorts of purposes. Why should any one of these ways reflect an indifferent, amorphous nature any more that any other? In other words, it is claimed that our type-hierarchies vary according to our local and current needs. Why should we think a type-hierarchy depicts an underlying ordering of real natural kinds?

Vision (1988) and Boyd (1990, 1991) have given detailed answers to the attack on the objective existence of natural kinds. In the first place, as Hacking points out (1991: 111), realism *vis à vis* natural kinds does not commit one to the belief that there is 'a unique best taxonomy in terms of natural kinds'. The belief that there are many orders of natural kinds is perfectly compatible with the claim that natural kinds are objective and carve nature at its joints. What type-hierarchy we choose to work with may depend on the type of problem we are trying to solve, the nature of the phenomenon under investigation, and so on. In fact:

[T]he realist can quite coherently accept the pluralist conception of scientific categories even within a single scientific discipline ... the realist could acknowledge that for every particular scientific program there is an infinite plurality of appropriate conceptual schemes that fit the causal structure of the world equally well and between which the choice is arbitrary. (Boyd, 1990: 189-90)

A crucial, first step in answering those who maintain a conventionalist stance to the categorising of nature while accepting the need for multifarious systems of classifications is to insist that each such system is constrained by the causal structure of the world.

Boyd (and earlier Bhaskar, 1973) have delivered the final blow to categorical conventionalism. Their argument is based on one very important and, to us, obvious fact: nature is intransigent and unforgiving. There are causal structures that exist independently of the theories and projects and beliefs of human kind, that are totally unaffected by the way we classify things (Boyd, 1990: 183). On the other hand, we have seen how these causal structures, through the laws that have been discovered experimentally, are implicated in the determination of type uniqueness. In other words, if the set of laws for each system is invariant under a transformation from one set of descriptive categories to another or from one type-hierarchy to another, then those laws capture, directly or indirectly a feature of the intransigent order of nature. A type-hierarchy that reflects those sets of laws is constituted from natural kinds that must exist independently of any human project or conceptual system. There will also be categorial systems that do survive the invariance test because their existence outside some human construction is not permitted by any set of laws.

The principle that any classification scheme must pay homage to the actual causal powers in nature does allow for a measure of convention to enter into the way we classify things but not in the way the conventionalist intended. Choice between competing schemes may be a matter of convention to the extent that each system is compatible with the actual causal structure of the world. If the choice between two conceptions is arbitrary (in particular, if it is conventional), then they reflect the causal structure of the world equally well (or badly) (Boyd, 1990: 183, 184).

Let us consider the above hierarchy of types of oscillators. Suppose one group of engineers classifies pendulums in terms of materials for their manufacture while another group does so according to certain aesthetic criteria. Both groups are designing grandfather clocks, but with different aspects of the finished product in mind. It should be clear that these systems of classification are compatible and the choice of which is to dominate in the design process is a function of the needs of the grandfather-clock business. But one and the same chunk of the oscillator hierarchy underlies both systems of classification.

Notice that the above example slips between natural and artificial kinds, with an intermingling of objective and conventional features in conceptual structure of the hierarchy. This is a common feature of actual hierarchies in use.

> [T]he definition of the kind 'gene' should possess few conventional features whereas the definition of the kind 'fish fork' should be largely arbitrary. It likewise follows that there should be kinds and categories whose definitions combine naturalistic and conventional features in quite complex ways. Consider the notion of having been legally married in New York State. Complex psychological notions like consent, deeply linked to induction and explanation, are involved in the legal definition of marriage, but so are notions with a high degree of arbitrariness – like being a properly ordained member of the clergy. (Boyd, 1991: 140)

We could also classify various pendulums in terms of colours to fulfil certain safety regulations or fashion fads, but such a classification can easily be incorporated into the above type-hierarchy, just as long as such a classification is compatible with the relevant laws. We have learned that natural kinds are classes whose membership is determined by the causal or lawlike relations among the basic particulars of our world. We have also learned that there are many ways in which a natural kind supertype can be realised. There will be as many different ways as there are versions of the law(s) of the supertype system, since the supertype is simply a representation of the sets of entities with properties in common that are picked out by the most general laws. For example, according to quark theory there are different kinds of protons in that different combinations of quarks possessing charge, spin, colour, etc., can constitute a proton. Yet, they all have the above general features in common. In our representation then a subset of the supertype set is formed for each different way the laws of the supertype apply, and these ways are expressible in terms of the boundary conditions that define each system. Each subset of entities is covered by its own, unique law.

To say, then, of a given object that it is a kind of thing means that the object in question is the same as one of the combinations or arrangements of objects represented by the relevant supertype, a combination or arrangement that is a way in which the common 'supertype' property is realised. It also means that the common subtype property is *identified* with the common supertype property. The identity, here, is between the macroscopic property common to the things represented by the subtype and a macroscopic property common to all the combinations of entities represented by the supertype.

Let us consider an imaginary example of this relationship between types. Suppose the universe consisted of only two kinds of fundamental particles each of which can possess one of only two properties. It can be positively or negatively charged. Suppose also that these particles exist only in pairs, the minimal physical systems. There would then be only four possible combinations: $+ -$, $- +$, $+ +$, $- -$. In other words, there are only four possible ways to be a system of fundamental particles. In addition to the charge properties, we have two types of 'macro' properties, that is properties of the pairs or systems. They can have a net charge of zero and a net charge of two. Now, suppose we have four other discrete macro properties: a disposition to appear red in standard circumstances, a disposition to appear green in standard circumstances and large or small. Sometimes a system is observed to be red, green, large or small but never any two of these at the same time (Figure 2.3).

We discover through experimentation that red and green things behave exactly the same way as zero net charge systems and large and small things behave exactly the same way as systems with a net charge of two. We conclude that red colour indicates the presence of the 'red' disposition of a macro individual which is numerically identical to the zero net charge of a micro combination. It would be rational to conclude that the

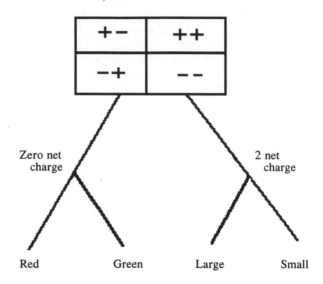

Figure 2.3. The structure of an imaginary fundamental theory

green colour of another object indicates the presence of a 'green' disposition, numerically identical with the zero net charge of a *different* micro combination. The red of the former system is not the same as the green of the latter, though both appear the way they do because they have zero net charge. They are identified with different inherent zero net charges since there are two ways for a system to have a zero net charge. In this imaginary world, 'red' systems and 'green' systems are members of the kind 'zero net charge systems'; they also happen to be different subkinds of the 'zero net charge' kind.

The same moves could be made for systems which appear to us as large and small. Large and small systems are distinguished by the different ways a macro system can have a net charge of two. So, large and small things are subkinds of the kinds of things that possess a net charge of two. Things that possess the two kinds of net charges are represented in the relevant type-hierarchy as subtypes of the ultimate supertype, and are identified with the four different combinations of fundamental particle pairs. Zero charge systems are either + − or − + micro combinations and systems of net charge two are either ++

or – – micro combinations. Property identity only holds for the individual properties of individual members.

How, then, do we represent these relationships between kinds using the apparatus of type-hierarchies and subtypes and their corresponding supertype? We construct a model universe. Subtypes are represented as disjoint sets; there are no attributes in common among them. The collecting of subtypes by a supertype is represented by a map: the domain of the map is the disjoint subtype sets while the range is the supertype set. More precisely, the domain consists of a set of ordered pairs, {<a,P>, <b,Q>, ..., <n,M>}, where the lower-case letters stand for individuals and the upper-case letters the property of that individual which it has in common with the other members of the set, property identity being one of the unanalysed primitives of our system. The same holds for the supertype range, {<u,R>, <v,T>, ..., <s,S>}. So ordered pairs of subtypes are mapped on to supertype pairs and the mapping function is the identity relationship e.g. <a,P> = <s,S>. The integrity of each subtype system is preserved by the fact that its law is a version of the general law of + and – particle combinations. Whether there are links between subtypes and supertypes is an empirical matter, a consequence of the fundamental laws of nature. It is not determined *a priori* by the imposition of a mathematical structure on an indeterminate array of properties.

The above identity relationship between the members of subtype and supertype sets in our model universe, which reflects or represents identity relations among the real entities of the world, enables us to avoid a Platonic proliferation of emergent natural kinds. The number of natural kinds is a function of the number of versions of the fundamental laws, while the scope of these laws determines supertype-subtype rankings.

5. How relations among natural kinds are reflected in the structure of type-hierarchies

It is our contention that the mathematical structure of a type-hierarchy should be motivated by the ordering of the natural kinds it is supposed to represent. Some researchers on semantic networks characterise a type-hierarchy as a Boolean lattice,

Realism Rescued

where the nodes denote classes and the links stand for class inclusion.

Such an approach will not work for our purposes. In the first place, a Boolean lattice structure (Figure 2.4) allows for too many interrelations between types of properties because for any pair of types there exists a minimal common supertype and a maximal common subtype:

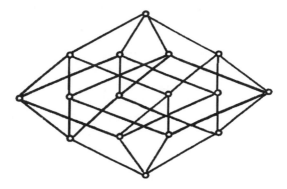

Figure 2.4. A Boolean format for type-hierarchies

But there seems to be no natural motivation for this, for some natural kinds are not specific cases of others; red is not a shape and square is not a colour. So we should not expect all the nodes in our representation to be interlinked. Even worse, a Boolean lattice requires a universal common supertype and a universal common subtype. In other words, a Boolean lattice *a priori* rules out the realistic possibility of more than one highest ranked supertype and several lowest ranked subtypes. The structure that best represents the actual ordering of types or natural kinds is known as a tangled hierarchy (Fahlman, 1979), i.e. a directed acyclic graph that has some branches that separate and come back again, permitting some nodes to have the same parent. Instead of a Boolean lattice, we have a kind of partial ordering of type nodes (Figure 2.5) (Fahlman, 1979: 17-24).

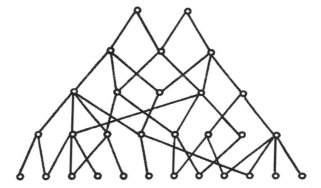

Figure 2.5. A partial ordering of type nodes

Notice that many of the nodes in the diagram lack either a common supertype or a common subtype which, we believe, reflects the actual ordering of type expressions in natural language. It allows for the possibility that there are more than one ultimate supertype and that the number of subtypes increases as we travel down the hierarchy, without having to converge into a single subtype.

In Chapter One we sketched our approach to the problem of the defence of scientific realism. We share with many philosophers of science the idea that at the heart of all scientific theories are models of the world. In the next three chapters we turn to the study of models in science. We begin with a naturalistic or descriptive treatment of models, which turns out to be incomplete in its dependence on the idea of analogy. Could deficiencies in the naturalistic analysis be made good by presenting the structure of modelling in terms borrowed from the way models are used in logic? This treatment is also incomplete, since it is insensitive to the ontological constraints on the selection of models in real science. In Chapter Five we show how the weaknesses in both treatments can be eliminated by the use of the notion of type-hierarchy.

CHAPTER THREE

A Naturalistic Analysis of the Use of Models in Science

1. Models and theories

The idea that theories are intimately involved with models has been a commonplace in the philosophy of science for generations. It has rarely gone unchallenged. Part of the unease some philosophers have felt with the ubiquitous role assigned to models by many of us comes from reflecting on the problem in terms of a different concept of model from that which realists have been using. It is essential then at the outset that we should describe the use of models in the physical sciences, in all their variety, so that there will be no ambiguity in our use of the expression.

Our starting point will be taken from a brief reflection on the nature and function of theories. There are many ways in which the role of theories can be discussed. We shall use the notion of a theory as a mapping, which links the members of one set of entities to those of another in a systematic way. The Cartesian or logicist account of theory, expressed in these terms, treats a theory as a mapping from propositions onto propositions. The domain of the mapping is the set of laws and definitions constitutive of the theory, and the range is the set of lowest-level logical consequences of the theory. The mapping relation is deduction. Even in its most sophisticated form as the well-known deductive-nomological treatment of theories this picture is so fraught with unwelcome and counter-intuitive consequences that it is scarcely worth spilling any more ink in exposing its deficiencies. An alternative, 'materialist' account of theory interprets a theory as a mapping from phenomena onto states of affairs. The latter are usually unobservable, but their kind or type is specified in the common ontology upon which the theory and all those that are members of a sequence of theories adduced to account for a common field of phenomena are based.

The most important thing of all about these mappings is that they permit individuals to be mapped onto individuals *and* types to be mapped onto types. But how is this mapping achieved?

By taking up the idea that theoretical discourses are about models rather than the world itself, we can answer this question. The answer runs as follows: the content of a theory consists of a set of paired models. One of the pair serves to represent the phenomena to be explained while the other represents the mechanism by which those phenomena are generated. In the case of the descriptive model, the representing relation is a combination of idealisation and abstraction, which in the case of the explanatory model is the degree of weighted similarity of relevant properties or features between the model and what it represents. We shall call this the 'verisimilitude' of the model. The content of a theory can develop in two ways. One or other of the two models initially required to create the content of a theory tends to develop in such a way as to take over the role of the other. We shall illustrate this aspect of the dynamics of theorising below. But we shall also see that these models, whether as a pair or as a unified picture, develop along another dimension. A theory becomes a theory-family as the models are themselves elaborated within the constraints set by the type-hierarchy which defines the common ontology of some field of scientific endeavour. This too we shall illustrate below.

We shall justify this answer by analysing some cases of scientific theorising to demonstrate that the above schema represents the best account of the work of the theoretician. It is for this reason that we call this analysis 'naturalistic'. In the development of the philosophical underpinnings of the analysis we shall eventually show how the naturalistic analysis is sustained by a formal structure, through which the content of a theory can be expressed at the highest level of abstraction as a segment of a type-hierarchy. However, before we proceed to illustrate the analysis from the history of science one or two further observations are in order. The structure we have in mind can be pictured in the following way (Figure 3.1):

Phenomena $=^1$ Descriptive $-$ T $-$ Explanatory $=^2$ Generative
model   model   mechanism
   where 'T' is a theoretical discourse.

Figure 3.1. The relations between constituent models

The relations '$=^1$' and '$=^2$' are idealisation/abstraction and verisimilitude respectively. It should be emphasised that they are relations of degrees of resemblance. The details in any particular case could be expressed in terms of weighted similarities and differences between the model and what it represents. By 'weighted similarities and differences' we mean similarities and differences ranked with respect to their relevance for an act of comparison. There is nothing mysterious about these relations since models and what they are representations of or abstractions from are entities of the same metaphysical status, namely, in a general sense, things.

The relation between 'T', the theoretical discourse, and the models it describes is 'internal'. That is, there is always a mutual adjustment so that the models fit the descriptions in the theory and the theory is modified so that it will always fit the models, as they are adjusted to maintain their fit with the real-world entities they resemble.

According to the naturalistic account of 'model insertion' descriptive models are used to simplify the phenomena. Explanatory models are used to fill a gap in our knowledge. In many cases the mechanisms that generate phenomena are not observable by the same means as the phenomena they produce. Explanatory models are introduced to represent, as accurately as possible, unknown mechanisms and processes. The history of science shows that technical advances have often made possible the examination of both sides of the matching pair, so to say, when some means has been found for observing or manipulating the mechanism itself.

At a later stage in the analysis we shall show that in many cases the paired descriptive and explanatory models are aspects or 'faces' of one, more fundamental general model. The general model appears as a descriptive abstraction when it 'adjoins' the phenomena and as a representation of the real causal substructure when it 'adjoins' that substructure.

In this naturalistic treatment we have tried to remain faithful to the practice of the scientific community, as least as it has developed since the sixteenth century. Elsewhere (Harré, 1986) we have argued that it has been a desideratum for a good theory that the descriptive and theoretical models should be capable of unification within the constraints of a common ontology. In the end the development of a science should lead to there being only one model, applied descriptively to simplify phenomena and applied explanatorily to account for them. Looked at in this way, what we have called the descriptive model and explanatory model are really functionally distinguished aspects ideally of just the one model. However, the history of science shows that the unification may be hard won and sometimes never fully achieved. In his account of the use of models Giere (1988) assumes the hard work done. He analyses theorising at the point at which the unification of descriptive and explanatory models has already been achieved.

The 'electron stream' model of electricity can be looked at abstractly as a mapping between observed electrical phenomena and certain unobserved states and processes which bring about the observed phenomena but whose nature is unknown. Both the phenomena and the processes which produce them are represented by models drawn from a common source, the idea of the 'electron stream'. There is one model with two faces. The condition of the gold leaves in a charged electroscope is represented as a distribution of negative and positive charges: that is, by a model which highlights certain features of the system under study. The charging and discharging of an electroscope is explained by the movements of these charges: that is, by a model of whatever process is actually occurring. In this case the unity of the models as aspects or uses of the same underlying model of electrical phenomena in general is obvious. However, the problem of the degree of verisimilitude of these faces or aspects to the realities with which they must be compared takes a different form in each case. In its role as a descriptive model the general model presents a face towards a set of phenomena whose characteristics are already known. The model in this aspect is merely a device for elegantly abstracting an idealisation of the phenomena from the messy world of the apparatus. It has the status of a description. But the face that presents itself to the unobservable states of affairs that underlie the phenomena is not an abstraction from those states of affairs nor are they projections of it. The degree of verisimilitude of the face that addresses the unknown must be discovered empirically. It has the status of a hypothesis. The general model for theorising about electrical phenomena is functionally differentiated into distinct aspects or faces.

When a theory involves a pair of models that are each related to a different type-hierarchy there will be competing ontologies. The development of the theory-family of which the doubly grounded theory is the starting point usually involves the absorption of one of the competing ontologies by the other. A nice example, for which we are indebted to James Horgan, is to be found in the history of models for the gas laws. Boyle made use of the generic concept of elasticity in conceiving of the 'gas spring' experiment through which he found the law that bears his name. Later, still within the system of types dominated by the idea of elasticity, Hales proposed an explanation for the shrinkage in volume of an enclosed sample of air during combustion. The volume was reduced by one fifth because the burning candle reduced the elasticity of the air by that amount. Hales believed that the effect was not due to the absorption of a constituent of the air conceived as a mixture of gases each of a distinct molecular type. On the other hand, during the nineteenth century, the molecular picture took over the role that Boyle's spring idea had played. But as it did so, it forced the scientists who used that model to admit certain identities between states and properties of the aggregates of moving particles as imagined in accordance with the molecular model, and the properties of gases as investigated by Boyle, Gay-Lussac, Amagat and others. Pressure *is* rate of change of momentum of the molecular entities at a phase boundary, the volume just *is* the free space available for molecular motion, and the temperature of the gas *is* the mean kinetic energy of the aggregate of molecules. Thus the molecular or corpuscularian model takes over both the explanatory and the abstractive or descriptive function.

2. What do scientific discourses describe?

The distinction between what is observable and what is not and between what is manipulable and what is not by a well-equipped human being are not, for the most part, epistemic distinctions in the practice of science. For theories which are neither abstract representations of natural processes and nothing else, such as Newtonian kinematics, nor at the final frontier of the sciences of an epoch, such as general relativity, the distinctions are technical/historical. It is in that sense that they apply to such entities as micro-organisms, metallic crystals, the moons of Uranus, Burges dislocations, tectonic plates, blood capillaries, stagnant films, interstellar 'jets' and so on. Whether examples of any or each of these kinds of beings can be observed or manipulated depends on the equipment available to a scientist, engineer or medical practitioner. And that differs from epoch to epoch. At a rough estimate theorising about such entities must be a thousand times more common than theorising about the kinds of entities that thrill most philosophers, such as Newtonian forces and quantum states. The kind of theories we are talking about occupy a band between the sciences of the routinely observable, such as classical geology, and the sciences of the deepest groundings of reality, such as high energy physics. They are on the fault-line between the phenomenological and the fundamental. They must be taken very seriously because theorising about objects that are concealed from us only by history and the state of technology is almost always involved in the transition of a science from one stage of development to another.

The idea of a model and of the relational property of type identity will be used as our metascientific concepts to reveal the fine structure of such middle-level scientific discourses as microbiology, metallurgy, geology, anatomy, astronomy and so on. It has long been realised that scientific discourses cannot be neatly partitioned into a descriptive part and a theoretical part. Nevertheless we do routinely talk of 'theories'. At this point in our analysis we will suspend the use of that expression in favour of the more general expression 'scientific discourse', returning to site the concept of 'theory' more precisely in the landscape of science.

Scientific discourse is intentional discourse. It is about something. It is directed towards certain classes of intentional objects. But which? It seems obvious that scientific discourse is and always has been about natural phenomena, their inner natures and their causes. Yet, when we pay close attention to the semantics of real scientific discourses this simple picture dissolves. There does seem to be a complex intentional 'object' underlying and giving meaning to scientific discourses, but it is poorly represented in the printed discourses of the standard forms of scientific literature, the journal article and the textbook. The one thing that this intentional object manifestly is *not* is the world as it exists independently of human beings and their languages and equipment. So what are we to make of our commitment to scientific realism?

We hold that scientific discourses are not about an independent world, but about models of certain aspects of that world. We refer to that world indirectly via our models and we understand it obliquely through our models. The key epistemological question for any science is the degree of resemblance between models and reality, or, as it is sometimes said, their verisimilitude. But would it not be necessary to have an independent view of reality to assess the degree of resemblance between models and world? We shall try to show that that searching question can be sidestepped, and that we can defend a version of realism that is not vulnerable to such an objection. At this point we shall proceed with a naturalistic account of the way models are used by scientists in their everyday activities.

3. The modelling relation analysed as type-identity

In this chapter we shall highlight the analogy relation in giving an account of what it is for something to be a model in use in a science. It is as analogues of real or imagined things and processes that models *at first present themselves*. As we shall show in Chapter Five, there is a deeper structure underlying every analogy, namely the type-hierarchy within which both model, source and subject are subtypes. We shall be discussing here only the properties and uses of iconic models. Such models are related to their subjects (that of which they are models) and to their sources (that on which they are modelled) by relations of similarity and difference in their material properties, but 'similarity' and 'difference' as critically elaborated in Chapter Two. There are also formal models in use in science which are based on isomorphisms of abstract structures between models and their sources and subjects.

Since iconic models depend on comparisons and contrasts of material properties it is often possible to build them in the laboratory or the engineering workshop and to experiment upon them directly. Civil engineers who are given the task of managing the flow of water and the silting of channels in river estuaries make hydrographic models, sometimes on a considerable scale, with real sand, clay and water. They then experiment on these iconic representations of the geography of a real land and seascape by sending water in and out many times a day, greatly accelerating the effects of the tides. Twenty years of tidal erosion can be modelled in a few days. Sometimes models cannot be realised in metal and wood, but nevertheless can be imagined as concrete things, and experimented upon in the imagination. The role of models in experimental science is so important that we shall describe an example in some detail.

It is difficult, if not impossible, to make an experimental study of the flow of heat from the hot gases in the fire tubes of a Babcock boiler to the circulating water (see Figure 3.2). Insertion of thermocouples between the tubes interferes with the pattern of convection currents in the water. An ingenious model was constructed that exploits the similarity between the processes of mass transfer from a solid to a circulating liquid and heat transfer from a hot surface to a liquid. The appropriate number of sticks of 'rock', a sugar-based confection widely available at English seaside resorts, are inserted in a tube (see Figure 3.2), and water circulated. After some time the sticks are withdrawn and their profiles examined. They have been differentially dissolved away in a fashion that can be related to the way that heat would have been transferred from hot tubes to the water circulating in the Babcock boiler. Sometimes it is sufficient simply to imagine the model, describe its features mathematically, and work out how it would behave in the relevant circumstances. For instance the internal circulation of the liquid in a droplet can be studied by imagining that the surface tension is due to an enclosing membrane, a rubber balloon. Lately a powerful blend of the concrete and the formal methods of model experimentation has been developed with enormous success by the use of computer graphics.

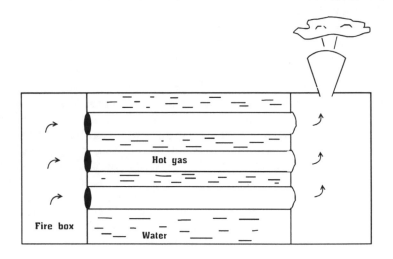

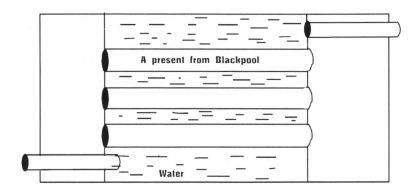

Figure 3.2. The Babcock boiler and its model

From a logical point of view experimenting with a model of a system and with a real system, whether the model is concretely or abstractly represented, differ as counterfactual situations differ from actual. Models are instruments that give us access to the behaviour of what we will call 'virtual worlds'. Model experimentation illustrates the crucial point that possibilities are of this world. Studying counterfactual states of affairs, that part of the extension of a law of nature inaccessible to the instrumentation with which we investigate what actually exists, is something we can do here and now. Sometimes we do it by running models on the laboratory bench, sometimes by graphic displays on the computer screen, sometimes by solving differential equations. We need no baroque ontology of possible worlds existing alongside this world to understand the nature of possibility in science.

4. The analogy structure of a model

We can now be a little more formal in specifying the conditions under which something 'A' can be an iconic model of something 'B', its subject. At this point in the analysis we shall express them in terms of the standard components of an analogy relationship.

(a) There shall be a positive analogy between A and B, i.e. A and B must be similar in the relevant respects. Of course what is to count as relevance is to be decided case by case, but as we shall show, that decision is never ad hoc.
(b) There may be a negative analogy between A and B, i.e. A and B may be different in certain respects, related to the relevance conditions of (a).
(c) There will probably be a neutral analogy, consisting of those properties of A whose mapping onto the properties of B has not been explored. We do not know whether they are similarities or differences.

If the neutral analogy is either empty or considered irrelevant to the purposes of the modelling, the analogy relation is symmetrical. In these circumstances A can be a model of (for) B and B can be a model of (for) A. An electrical circuit can be a model of a hydraulic network and a hydraulic network can be a model for an electrical circuit. Since we have required there to be a negative analogy between a model and what it models the modelling relation cannot be reflexive, a thing cannot be a model of itself. Relative to the relevance considerations of the case it is sometimes possible for the modelling relation to be transitive. That is if A is a model of (for) B, and B is a model of (for) C, then A is a model of (for) C. A water-filled balloon can be a model for a droplet and a droplet can be a model for an atomic nucleus, so *ceteris paribus* a water-filled balloon can be a model of an atomic nucleus.

It follows from these considerations that nothing is a model as such. An entity is a model considered with respect to its relations to something else. 'Model' is a use concept. In practice the symmetry between a model and its subject is ruled out by the existence or acknowledgment of a neutral analogy.

So far we have specified only the model-to-subject relation. But we shall not understand the structure of model-making without paying attention to the sources of models. The source is that which a model is modelled on. For those models which are created by abstraction from phenomena, those we have called 'descriptive', the source of the model is the same entity, process etc. which is its subject. But for those we have called 'explanatory' the subject of the model is the unknown process or entity involved in the causal substructure of the phenomena to be explained. *A fortiori* the source of such a model must be something other than its subject. For instance the general Newtonian material particle is the source of the molecular model of gases. We shall show how these model-subject-source relations can be expressed in terms of locations within the structure of a type-hierarchy. It follows from that that the use of the relation of (material) analogy in describing how models are to be understood does not capture the underlying structure of the knowledge-representation system within which such analogy relations can be identified. The underlying relation between a model, its source and its subject, by virtue of which they display mutual analogies, is that they are subtypes of the same supertype. It is this fact about models that serves as the constraint on the natural kinds that they can represent.

5. The fine structure of the content of some middle-level theories

One must assume that common experience is first differentiated and categorised by the use of some loosely organised common-sense schemes, scarcely well integrated or simple enough to be described as sciences. There are no brute facts, though for each such scheme there are phenomena which cannot be further analysed or recategorised. Further refinement of the abstractions from such phenomena requires the use of supplementary schemes. Many of these take the form of analogues. They sharpen our grasp of the patterns that are implicit in the phenomena or that can be made to emerge from it. They require us to take account of similarities and differences we might otherwise have overlooked. An analogue used for such a purpose is the source of a descriptive model. The effect of taking a sample of gas as analogous to a spring is to bring both the trapped gas and coils of wire under the same general category, 'spring'. In this way we reach a descriptive model of the gas sample, by which only those properties required to fill out the 'spring' idea are considered in the subsequent research. Hearing the calls of birds as 'songs' draws attention to the repeated melodic and rhythmic structure of the cries. The young Darwin looked at the bewildering diversity of plants and animals, both living and extinct, with the eyes of an English countryman. He constructed an abstract, descriptive model of the natural world by treating it as a subtype of the supertype to which both farms and stretches of a Galapagos forest belonged. He saw lines of descent, blood ties and so on where Captain Fitzroy saw instances of the creative munificence of God.

The value of any particular model source in constraining the way a descriptive model of phenomena abstracts and idealises them can emerge only in the fate of the research programme that it makes possible. The 'theory of signatures' was just such a failure. The salient properties of the fruit, flowers and so on, taken as a divine indication of their human use, did not in practice have the effects they should have. Despite their resemblance to the brain, walnuts have no cerebral virtues. Boyle's 'spring' model is still fruitful, and so is the 'agricultural' point of view with the help of which Darwin formed his picture of the interrelations of species. Goffman (1969) asked his readers to look on the loose groupings of people that act together in every-day life as 'teams', intent on managing certain impressions in the eyes of others. This famous simile brings out aspects of the behaviour of all sorts of people, including nurses and reception-ists at health clinics, that would have been difficult if not impossible to discern without Goffman's potent image. In our way of putting the matter Goffman treated the group of nurses and doctors who work in a clinic as a subtype of the supertype 'team' of which such groups as the Red Sox are also subtypes.

In the day-to-day practice of science, with which we are now concerned, there is no surety that the explanatory models con-structed to represent the unknown causal substructure of the systems whose nature and behaviour has been successfully represented in various descriptive models will be based on the very same source as those descriptive models. In the case of the behaviour of gases the descriptive model was based on the spring and the explanatory model on the Newtonian particle. The higher-order fusion of the two into a coherent virtual world or common model was a long time coming. About two hundred years separated Boyle's experiments from Clerk Maxwell's final synthesis. However, there are examples of developing sciences in which a common ontology expressed in a common virtual world drew on one and only one source for both modelling operations. Once again, as we shall show in Chapter Five, this can be best expressed in terms of the gradual bringing together of these 'elements' into a single type-hierarchy, and that is how an ontological synthesis of a field of seemingly disparate theories is achieved.

J.B. van Helmont, writing in the early part of the seventeenth century, based his theory of disease on the idea of an invading army. The body, he proposed, is infected by an incursion of alien *archeae*, hostile powers, which take over the bodily organs for their own purposes. In so doing they produce toxic wastes which are the causes of the symptoms. The same source is used to manage the abstraction and idealisation of the observed disease syndrome, that is to create the descriptive model, and to manage the invention of an iconic, explanatory model to represent the unobservable causal substructure of the disease. As subtypes of the same supertype these models are ontologically coherent. This pair of models developed into the nineteenth-century conception of the bacterial model. It displaced various other pictures of the nature of diseases, such as the poison theory encapsulated in the etymology of the word 'mal-aria', bad air. Pasteur enriched the explanatory model by treating yeasts, which he had studied during his time in the wine industry, and the bacteria infecting the diseased patient, as of the same natural kind. This final step made a clearly defined programme of research into microbial agents possible.

We have remarked on Darwin's use of the farm as the source of his descriptive models of a complex array of species in the natural world. He used the same source to construct his explanatory model representing the causal substructure of the patterns he had discerned in that world. The steps that lead up to the concept of 'natural selection' are managed through the treatment of the domestic selection of plants and animals as the same kind of process as their natural selection. The first part of Darwin's argument is occupied with detailed descriptions of the breeding of plants and animals domestically, together with a discussion of the variations that appear in successive generations. The upshot of these reflections could be expressed in a kind of 'formula':

Domestic variation acted on by domestic selection leads to domestic novelty (that is to new breeds and varieties).

As the second chapter unfolds Darwin takes his readers through a great many examples of natural variation and natural novelty, the appearance of new species. We are carried along by the narrative to the point where we are driven to contemplate another 'formula':

Natural variation acted on by ...?... leads to natural novelty (that is to new species).

The rhetorical force is irresistible and we find ourselves making Darwin's great conceptual leap ourselves. The unknown and unobservable mechanisms of speciation must 'be' natural selection. Of course the 'being' of this process is, in the first instance, as an explanatory model, creating a virtual world in which we can 'see' species evolving.

The reasoning is type-hierarchical, and as the theory-family of Darwinian and neo-Darwinian evolutionary explanations developed the limits of the analogy came to be examined through explicit statements of the likenesses and differences between the subtypes of the 'selectionist' supertype. Darwin himself systematically deleted some of the common implications of the term 'selection' from his scientific use of the concept. His deletions included any implications of volition and of planning and direction that the concept normally includes.

The basic structure of any scientific 'virtual world' derives from the exigencies of explanation. In a great many cases the descriptive models represent patterns in phenomena for the explanation of which the community may be at a loss. The deficit is made good by imagining causal mechanisms which would produce such patterns in phenomena. But in the first instance the real mechanisms are unobservable. There is no direct check on the verisimilitude of the iconic models built to stand in for them. In some cases the possibility of an observational test can be indefinitely postponed. Shall we ever come close to an observational test of the three-quark model of subatomic particles? The community cannot tell what is producing the phenomena of interest by touching, tasting, looking or hearing what is going on 'behind the scenes', so to speak. It is to remedy the lack of 'microscopical eyes', as Locke put it, that the controlled imagining of iconic model-building is required. The role of the common ontology, specifying the acceptable sources of explanatory models, is essential to this cognitive activity. Only plausible models, which fall under possible natural kinds, could be candidates for comparisons with how the world really is. If scientists are aiming at eventually making such comparisons, then the imagination must be constrained.

Looked at this way, a naturalistic analysis of the methodology of theorising goes something like this:

(1) Methodological step: a descriptive model is abstracted from the complex phenomena of nature.
(2) Ontological principle: observed patterns in phenomena are caused by unobservable productive processes.

(3) Methodological principle: a descriptive model of an observed phenomenon can be imagined to be caused by an explanatory model standing in for the process by which the observed phenomenon is caused.

(4) Methodological step: an explanatory model of the real productive process is constructed in accordance with the common ontology, that is a subtype of a supertype whose other subtypes include entities and processes which we already have reason to believe exist.

We have illustrated how this procedure creates a semantically organised theory-family for the explanation of an observed pattern of phenomena. It can be extended to explaining the sets of properties characteristic of material substances, by modelling their inner constitutions. However, it is important to point out that the semantics of theorising is intralinguistic. The meanings of the expressions that appear in explicit discourses of theoreticians describing some aspect of the virtual world of the theory are created within that world itself.

Within this structure there are three similarity relations which should be achieved.

(1) The descriptive model should fall under the same supertype as the observed phenomenon.

(2) The behaviour of the model of the real productive process should be qualitatively identical to the behaviour of the mechanisms of that real process (which we know since it is the very phenomenon we wish to explain!). This is the behavioural criterion of model adequacy.

(3) The natural kind of the explanatory model should be of the same general type as the natural kinds specified in the common ontology. This could be called the 'material criterion', following Hesse's terminology.

The behavioural and material criteria control the way the community conceives an explanatory model as a hypothetical generative mechanisms which would, were it real, produce the phenomenal patterns represented by the relevant descriptive model. It is important to emphasise that hypothetical generative processes, so conceived, are, strictly speaking, representations of whatever the real productive mechanisms might be. It is now obvious, we hope, that the question of the degree of resemblance between the hypothetical mechanism represented in the explanatory model and the real mechanism is *the* question for the defender of scientific realism. We know how the real mechanism behaves. We imagine, through the joint constraints expressed in the behavioural and material criteria for adequacy of models what that mechanism might be like. These relationships have already appeared in the preliminary sketch of the structure of the whole theoretical complex laid out in the first section of this chapter (Figure 3.1).

6. The plausibility and implausibility of theories

The next step in our naturalistic analysis of scientific theorising will be to give an account of the plausibility or implausibility of theories, in terms of the structure of the virtual worlds constituted by the paired models which represent the content of those theories. We shall argue in a later chapter that the plausibility of a theory, as we shall define it, is one of the two major inductive grounds for giving that theory a realist construal, that is for coming to believe that the models, that taken jointly constitute the virtual world of the theory resemble the structure of the real world. At the same time that belief can serve as the ground for deciding on an experimental project, to explore the world for exemplars of the types of entities incorporated in the paired descriptive and explanatory models, to check the degree of resemblance between the models and what they represent.

Expressing the content of a theory-family in terms of a sequence of developing models and their sources in a common ontology contrasts sharply in its degree of explicitness with the customary way of writing science. In the discursive presentation of a theory only a small part of the total content in expressed. Usually it is only the hypothetical generators and the descriptive model that are described. The common ontology and the pre-abstraction phenomena are usually omitted. We are not informed as to what system of natural kinds (i.e. what type-hierarchy) the theorising is based on. It is simply taken for granted that the community shares a common ontology. However, there are some notable exceptions. When great scientific innovators such as

Darwin or Hales write up their work much more of the implicit cognitive resources of the community come to be laid out explicitly. To appreciate the basis of judgments of plausibility and implausibility the full content of a theory-family must be attended to.

The content that is partly expressed in the successive members of a theory-family develops in response to two kinds of external pressures. There are new experimental results which must be assimilated, and the content of the theory-family must be adjusted to accommodate them. In accordance with our analysis new experimental results are contributions to our knowledge of the behaviour of the unknown causal mechanisms operating in the area of nature we are studying. New results are accommodated by adjustments to the behavioural analogy between the explanatory model and what it represents, which, in their turn, spark off adjustments in the material analogy between those models and their sources in the common ontology. Chemical valencies are at first related only to the proportions of atomic constituents of molecules. But the series of similarly constituted hydrocarbons could be accommodated in chemical theory only by adjusting the valency model, by including spatial orientation in the characteristics of valency bonds. But there are also changes in the theoretical background to the theory-family which come about by further developments in the explanatory model as it shifts in its relation to the common ontology. This is a change in the internal structure of the underlying type-hierarchy. Changes in one's views as to what natural kinds there are, in turn lead to changed expectations of the behaviour of the explanatory model and so to changes in the content of the behavioural criterion. And this prompts new experimental researches. A beautiful example of such a linked series of changes is the reasoning behind the programme for the experimental search for the W and Z particles. The common ontology of all quantum field theories is the general photonic 'object'. As the models of field interactions drew on and developed the fact that both kinds of intermediate vector 'particles' were subtypes of the same supertype, namely the general photonic object, new possibilities of phenomena displaying the marks of new free particles opened up (Brown and Harré, 1990). We shall be following through the details of this pattern of reasoning in the chapter devoted to our theory of properties. In the chapters to come we shall show how the formal properties of these changing relations can be expressed in terms of the structures of type-hierarchies and the locations in those hierarchies of the models and natural kinds to the naturalistic analysis of which we have devoted this chapter.

A theory is plausible if its descriptive and explanatory models are fully adjusted to the current range of experimental results and to the current conception of the common ontology. The more plausible a theory the greater, we shall argue, is its verisimilitude over rivals from the same theory-family. The less successfully can the models be adjusted the less plausible is the theory and the lesser its verisimilitude.

7. The sources of explanatory models

So far we have left the sources of explanatory models and so the all-important material relations at the heart of theories unanalysed. The role of the common ontology in the creation of a theory-family is to provide and maintain a set of natural kind rules in accordance with which the hypothetical entities that make up the explanatory models are to be designed. Bacteria, as an explanatory model of the causes of diseases, are a kind of organism, in particular a micro-organism. But for a realist construal of the use of such imagined entities to control an experimental programme for seeking concrete exemplars of bacteria, a mode of reference must also be given. We need to know where to look for them, and how to pick them out. Here we have recourse again to natural kind concepts. We believe that all natural kind concepts include a tacit ontological component which can be looked at, if we wish, as specifying a mode of reference to exemplars of the kind in question. For those natural kinds which are material things, that mode of reference is spatio-temporal, to a place at a time. Common ontologies as the progenitors of natural kind rules, if they are to suggest and control real-world searches, must incorporate prescriptions of determinate modes of reference. It turns out that that is just how common ontologies are structured. Domestic selection (drawn from the generic picture of nature as a farm) is the source for the model of natural selection. This constrains the ontology of the mechanism of speciation to 'material process'. Its one-time rival as a source of a model for the process of speciation, divine creation, standing as the supertype to which all subtypes must conform, constrained the ontology of the mechanism of speciation to 'intentional acts'. Once the ontological status of the model entities has been fixed, the subsidiary natural kind rules determine, in a general way, the features to be looked for in deciding whether a putative specimen should be recognised as a member of the kind in question. The common ontology then plays a central role in the setting up of search procedures that are consequential on a realist reading of a theory, and whose successes, we shall be arguing in a later chapter, are the basis on which the inductive argument for scientific realism ultimately rests.

Natural-kind constraints expressed in the underlying type-hierarchy determine the feasibility of the experimental projects associated with any theory-family. But they do more. They point the way ahead for the necessary technology. For instance, if the iconic explanatory model for the cause of disease is a *micro*-organism the appropriate instrument for use in a search for an exemplar would be a *micro*-scope. If natural selection is the iconic explanatory model for speciation we need a way of speeding it up by raising the selection pressure. If the iconic explanatory model for the core of Halley's comet is a rock about the size of the island of Sark we need to develop space probes with the ability to rendezvous with something hard and impenetrable.

So far our examples of cases of explanatory models and the features of these models that meet the behavioural and material criteria of model adequacy and their common ontologies have been chosen from among those that have been outstandingly successful, both in generating new concepts and in controlling search procedures. This we call the 'induction over types'. We shall return to this important feature of scientific development in the final argument of Chapter 9. The theory-families we have used as examples have developed through stages of increasing plausibility. But these are empirical methods. There are characteristic ways in which middle-level theories can go wrong. We shall illustrate this with an example from our own scientific work.

In our collective study (Marsh, Rosser and Harré, 1977) we tried to bring together under a single pair of linked models, that is under a single supertype, a cluster of empirical studies of violent and seemingly violent public behaviour. Marsh had made a detailed study of football hooliganism and Rosser had investigated a number of aspects of trouble in school. These studies were able to be fitted in to the structure of models typical of the 'ethogenic' approach to social psychology.

(1) The descriptive model is drawn from Goffman (1964). He suggested that it is often fruitful to treat and analyse an episode and the patterns of behaviour of those involved as of the same type as a dramatic production, a stage play. With the help of this idea a descriptive model of the events that occurred in and near football grounds could be abstracted, and the structures of 'hooliganism' displayed. Similarly, violent outbreaks in schoolrooms could be seen as ritualised and orderly sequences of social acts.

(2) Coordinate with the dramaturgical models with which the structure of the phenomena had been displayed we proposed an explanatory model drawn from the same common ontology: that is, as falling under the same supertype in the underlying type-hierarchy. The actions of those taking part could be explained as if they were of the same type as those of actors following a script. This 'picture' was developed in contrast to other explanatory models drawn from other sources, such as the ethological model in which violent interactions were seen as of the same type as the status battles of male animals.

A theory-family began to develop around the transfer of the concept of 'rule', displaced from contexts in which rules are explicit and known to the actors. In its explanatory role a rule system could not be taken to be explicitly known. An increasingly problematic dissimilarity began to appear as differences between the concept of 'rule' and whatever it was that was responsible for orderly social behaviour were explored: that is, it became less and less plausible to treat them as subtypes of the same supertype. This led to a growing dissatisfaction with the explanatory power of the concept of 'rule' and thus with the explanatory role-rule model as these had crystallised in the research. The dissatisfaction was ontological. Does it make sense to suppose that there exist rules in the minds of social actors, which render them capable of orderly interactions? It came to seem as if the answer was 'no'.

8. Theory-families and their virtual worlds as systems

Finally we want to emphasise the 'system' character of what we have been describing. By that we mean that theories and their models are so structured and interrelated that equilibrium can be restored if the structure is disturbed by some outside influence. The explanatory model at the heart of the content of the explanatory part of the relevant theory is tied to observed natural patterns by its place in a type-hierarchy. How it is imagined to behave in accordance with its nature must be similar, in the relevant respects, to how the real but unknown causal mechanisms behave. But, as we have pointed out above, the further pursuit of an experimental programme, or sometimes just some accidental discovery, may throw up patterns of behaviour that disturb that placement of subtypes and supertypes. For instance, when Amagat investigated the behaviour of gases under very high pressures the relationship between pressure and volume expressed in Boyle's Law no longer held. He describes how he then proceeded. In our terms he reflected on the explanatory model, the gas as a swarm of molecules drawn from the Newtonian particle as a primary source. The 'molecule' of the then extant theory was but a point-particle. But the source entity, representing the common ontology that defined the theory-family, had volume too. By relocating the molecule type at a different point in the material type-hierarchy, he added 'volume' to the properties of the gas molecule. At high pressures this molecular volume, say b, becomes a significant factor in the free space available for molecular motion in this model. So the volume term for the renovated Boyle's Law must be $(V-b)$. And so it proved. The structure of the whole complex, models and common ontology, is a system and self-restoring, since all the models are subtypes of the same supertype.

CHAPTER FOUR

Some Proposals for the Formal Analysis of the Use of Models in Science

1. A summary of the naturalistic treatment of the uses of models in physical science

Cosmologists create equations which describe imagined models of the universe – in the sense of imagined entities which are representations of the universe 'in reality': that is, as it might be thought to exist independently of human beings. But notice that we speak here of how the universe is 'thought to exist', and that implicates human categories in the very act of thinking. Nevertheless though the universe in itself, so to speak, is not and could not be given to us in the same way as the model, we do take the model to represent 'it'. From time to time some of these models have been given concrete form as elegant pieces of machinery: for instance, the once popular orreries, and the gadgetries of planetaria and so on. Perhaps most interesting of all the possible models of the cosmos are the motets for seven voices in Kepler's *Harmonices mundi*. These devices illustrated or, as we should now say, interpreted mathematical descriptions of heavenly movements. They scarcely ever served as research tools. In the last few years a model of the universe has been constructed from liquid crystal systems which does serve as a research tool (Peterson, 1991). This is the Zarek-Turok-Yulke phase transition model, described by Turok as follows: 'the system is quite analogous to the early universe case. It's a concrete system where you can really test some of the ideas that have developed for understanding defects in the early universe', that is, symmetry breaking phase transitions. We have called physical systems of this sort 'homoeomorphic' models. They are analogous in their behaviour to some real system but are known not to be ontologically plausible representations of it.

Woods (1977) describes the methods of Kelvin and Maxwell as follows: 'analogies assumed to exist were translated into hypothetical physical mechanisms, which, it was hoped, imitated nature sufficiently to be considered "real". A physical model was thus an induction from observation, aided by imagination, experience and luck.' Maxwell was largely responsible for two of the most potent models used in nineteenth-century physics, the molecular model described by the kinetic theory of gases and the tubes of force model described by his laws of electromagnetism. It was clear to Maxwell that the tubes of force were not representations of the real mechanisms responsible for electromagnetic phenomena. 'I do not bring it forward as a mode of connection existing in nature, or even as that which I would willingly assent to as an electrical hypothesis,' he said. The case was very different for the molecular model of gases. The Maxwell-Boltzmann model of 'small bodies or groups of smaller molecules repelling each other has come to be taken as a more and more accurate representation of the real nature of gases'. Both kinds of model fall under Gauss's concept of 'construirbare Vorstellung': that is, 'constructible representation' (Santema, 1978).

The question of the resemblance between a model and its real counterpart seems to be of the first importance in assessing theories and independent of the predictive power (empirical adequacy) of the theory that is created by describing that model. Throughout this work we would like to shift the emphasis from the old question 'How do we know our theoretical statements are true?' to 'How do we know whether and to what extent our models resemble (represent) structured existents which have their being independently of human languages, practices and modes of perception?'

From a naturalistic analysis of the content of scientific theories we derive the thesis that a theory is a description of a triad of entities. There is the explicit idealised representation of the phenomena to be explained. There is the implicit iconic representation of the 'mechanism' generating the phenomena. Thirdly, there is the source upon which that iconic representation is modelled. We have called these the descriptive,

explanatory and source models respectively. As we shall show
in the next chapter, the internal structure of the triad can be
displayed through the 'placement' of the types exemplified in
each of the three models in a type-hierarchy. The notion of
'model' has been central to the naturalistic criticism of the
deductive-nomological or pure sentential account of theories
since the early 1960s. Of course the need to include the content
of theories in any philosophical treatment of science had been
realised much earlier by Campbell (1920 [1957]). Though he did
not use the word 'model', his treatment of theory content was
very similar to that offered by the naturalists. The question to
be addressed in this chapter is whether a formal treatment of
theory content, understood along the lines of the naturalistic
analysis, is possible, and if so whether it serves any useful
philosophical purpose.

Can an abstract formal presentation of the models account of
the content of scientific theories be developed? The 'naturalists'
have, until recently, seen little point in the attempt. The failure
of the deductive-nomological account of scientific theorising
seemed to some to be an illustration of the pointlessness of
formal treatments. However, since we wish to propose our own
semi-formal treatment of a model-structure account of the content of scientific discourses in terms of type-hierarchies we must
take into consideration the recent attempt at formal analysis. It
preserves the modellers' basic insight but depends on the abstract notion of 'model' taken from logic and expressed in terms
of set theory.

In the 'naturalistic' literature the word 'theory' has been used
in its usual sense, namely as a discourse about models of the
world. The content of such a discourse is given by its model
structure, as an evolving 'cognitive object'. The best-known
attempt to develop a formal treatment of the model structure
which is the content of scientific discourse is the 'structural' or
'non-statement' account of Sneed (1971) and Stegmuller (1979).
In their treatment the word 'model' retains some of the same
range of uses as it has in the writings of naturalist analysts such
as Hesse (1961) and Toulmin (1956). The notorious difficulty in
understanding the non-statement treatment stems in part from
a poor presentation, but in part from an idiosyncratic use of the
word 'theory'. Formalists tend to refer to the set of models as the

'theory', and this leads to considerable confusion. There is no word left with which to refer to discourses about those models.

There are certain difficulties in trying to assess the value of the 'non-statement' treatment. It seems to have been proposed and developed independently of the main-stream work based on the naturalistic analysis of the role of models. Indeed there is almost no cross-referencing from the writings of Sneed, Stegmuller and Molines to the very extensive 'naturalistic' literature. The problem of assessment is twofold. How are the technical expressions of the formalists to be interpreted? There are terms like 'intended application' and 'constraint' which refer to important features of the account but are never clearly explained, nor illustrated with an adequate diet of examples. Does the formalist approach, once understood, offer any new insights into the procedures of science that were not already achieved by the naturalist approach?

Our first step will be to try to clarify the somewhat muddled terminology with which the notion of 'model' is introduced into logic, and from whence it is taken by the formalists. We shall highlight the similarities and differences with the way the naturalistic school understand the role of models in physics. Only then will we be in a position to provide a gloss on the terminology of the formalist school that will allow us to assess its value.

2. The use of the concept of 'model' in logic and mathematics

a. The standard use: models and the interpretation of calculi

The concept of 'model' is used in logic in the following way: the formulae of any abstract calculus are in need of interpretation into meaningful sentences. This can be done by choosing a semantic basis which will consist of some suitable 'universe' of objects with their characteristic properties and relations. This 'universe' can be made to serve as a source of meaning for the variables, connectives and constants of the calculus. We shall call such a set of objects and relations a 'semantic basis'.

In logical studies the meaning-creating relation through which a semantic basis becomes the source of meaning for the symbols of a calculus seems usually to be taken to be simple denotation. This step in the use of a semantic basis is rarely highlighted and even more rarely discussed explicitly. We have been unable to find any commentaries on the consequences for the interpretation of logics of building meaning in this way. Logicians have no settled terminology to describe this initial step.

A semantic basis is called a model for the calculus if and only if the sentences of the interpretation, when used to describe that semantic basis, are all true. There is, so to say, an 'internal' relation between the model and the statements made about it with the interpreted sentences of the calculus. The logician's usage is nicely exemplified by Bridge (1977: 34) who says, 'When O [a set of formulae interpreted by reference to U] is valid in U we say U is a *model* for O'. According to Bridge the letter 'U' denotes a 'relational structure' which consists of a set of elements, some of which can be individuated, and various relations that obtain among the elements. These relational structures are also sometimes called 'realisations'. It is important to emphasise that 'U' is entitative, not sentential. The word 'valid' in Bridge's definition comes as a surprise. One would expect that 'valid' would be reserved for correctly performed logical operations, with 'true' as the appropriate term for interpreted formulae used to make statements about the semantic basis. On pp. 33-4 Bridge offers 'true' as a synonym for 'valid'. We shall use 'true' in this context.

There are other unfortunate and confusing choices of terminology appearing in the writings of logicians. By flagging a particularly troublesome one we hope that confusion can be avoided. It concerns the use of the word 'interpretation'. For example, Mendelsohn (1987) says, 'an interpretation M is said to be a *model* for a set [A] of wffs if and only if every wff in [A] is true of M'. In English the word 'interpretation' is reserved for the result of interpreting something, not as that which facilitates the interpretation. In the next paragraph Mendelsohn goes on to say that an interpretation of M consists of a non-empty set D, called the domain of the interpretation, with relations, operators and fixed elements. This seems to mean that an interpretation in his sense, is entitative, not sentential. In short it is what we have called a semantic basis.

Logicians, so far as we can discern, have no interest in the external liaisons of any of the semantic bases which they use in their studies. Adequacy for the job in hand, which is more often than not testing for the consistency of the formal system in question, seems to be the sole criterion for choice of semantic basis. So far as we can see there is no attention to ontological considerations with respect to the viability of a semantic basis that will serve as a model.

b. Models in physics, taken formally

Models in physics can be seen as a species of the same genus of models as those that are used in logic. In physics the statements that can be made by the use of the sentences of an interpreted mathematical formalism are true of the semantic basis by the use of which the formulae of the mathematics were interpreted. The semantic basis must therefore count as a model, in the logician's sense, for the abstract mathematical formalism. For instance, the statement 'P (pressure).V (volume) = 1/3n (molecular number).m (molecular mass).c^2 (root mean square molecular velocity)' is true of a swarm of point molecules. But the interpretation of the formula 'pv=1/3nmc^2' as a sentence capable of being used to make the above statement requires the variables and constants of that formula to have been given meaning in terms of a 'world' of imagined material entities, the model. No gap could open up between the model and the statements of the theory, taken in its usual sense as a discourse, for which, as the relevant semantic basis, it provides the interpretation. If one or more of the statements made with an interpretation about a semantic basis should turn out to be false, it shows that that semantic basis ought not have been used to interpret the abstract formulae of the mathematics of the theory. False statements can appear in physics because some of the statements of the theory, the interpreted calculus, can be subject to experimental trial. In these circumstances physicists change the semantic basis in just such a way that a revised version of the original statement, seemingly empirically true, is also true of the new basis, which then becomes the current model. The basic principles governing the relation between abstract calculus, interpreted sentences and semantic basis as model are the same in physics and in model-theoretic studies in logic.

There are, however, some important differences. In the construction of a physical theory the model is almost always picked before the mathematical version of the theory is created. More often than not the abstract formalism of the mathematical version is developed just by describing the pre-existing model in formal terms. From a logical point of view the molecular model is the semantic basis for interpreting formulae such as '$pv=1/3nmc^2$'. But from the point of view of scientific methodology and the history of the kinetic theory the model was proposed first, probably most explicitly by Francis Bacon. It was progressively more carefully formulated and fully described in mathematical terms by Maxwell.

We have already remarked on the fact that logicians show little interest in the ontological or 'external' aspects of their models. A closer examination of how semantic bases are actually used in physics reveals that they are subject to external constraints. Physicists require that a theory should be physically meaningful: that is, the model for a theory should be physically plausible. Of all the range of entitative systems any one of which could be the semantic basis for the interpretation for the abstract mathematics of a theory only those models are selected which are similar in physically significant ways to entitative systems which are known to exist and about which physicists already know a great deal. The current model for electric circuitry is a special case of a hydraulic system. About such systems a good deal is known. This has been called the 'plausibility constraint' on the choice of models for physical theory. Hesse refers to it as the 'material analogy'. From a philosopher's point of view the plausibility constraint can be further analysed as we shall demonstrate in the next chapter in which we shall show how the ontology of specific models is constrained by their places in type-hierarchies.

From our point of view the only useful borrowing of the concept of 'model' from the formal sciences is from model-theory in logic. However, there is another use for the term 'model' in mathematics, which has been taken up by some philosophers of physics. Mathematicians sometimes call one formal system a model of another if there is a mapping which correlates the formulae of one system with those of another. There are 'models' of this sort to be found in the discourses of physicists (Redhead, 1980). However, it is difficult to see that they have any significance with respect to substantive issues in the philosophy of science. The fact that one can find rules to read one set of formulae into another parallel set tells us nothing about the possible meanings of sentences which could be derived from either of these sets of formulae. It tells us nothing about the physical plausibility of either. However, if the parallel set already has a model in the sense of a semantic basis it seems clear that the mapping between the sets of formulae would, more often than not, permit transitivity of modelling, *ceteris paribus*. Whatever is a model (semantic basis) for one system could also serve as a model (semantic basis) for the other. For instance, the formal mapping of the laws of hydraulic networks on to the laws of electric circuits permits the use of the 'current' model as a semantic basis for the latter.

The standard use of the word 'model' is exemplified by Del Rey (1974). 'A simplified treatment based on a model involves replacement of the actual physical system (say a molecule) by a simpler one (the model) which is treated in a quite rigorous way.' However, Redhead's account of the use of a 'model' to achieve the virtues of simplification (Redhead 1980: 147) runs as follows: 'In such a case [a theory too complicated for easy development] a simplified model M may be employed ... M plays the role of an *impoverished* theory, the important ingredient being that M and T contradict one another.' Only propositions can contradict one another. Redhead's use of the term 'model' is clearly not the standard use. It seems to belong with the specialised use in mathematics. Redhead uses the term in its common use just once. On pp. 149-50 (n. 5) he writes of the 'billiard ball model of a gas', though he does not continue in this vein. One can focus one's attention on a closed cycle of mathematical forms to the exclusion of the investigation of what gives them meaning as physical theories and what determines their plausibility as statements about the world. But this is to opt out of the philosophy of physics altogether.

3. Summary of the argument so far

Scientific discourses, fragments of which are picked out as theories, are about models and get their meaning from models. Models, in this sense, are a special case of the kind of models that are used by logicians. There are many similarities between the use of models in physics and their use in logic, but there are also many differences.

There are at least the following similarities:

(1) The interpretative role: both provide a 'vocabulary' with meaning, that is transform a formal or mathematical system into a theory: that is, into an intelligible discourse.
(2) The internal coherence role: in both cases statements made with the interpreted sentences of the theory are true of the model. Semantic bases leading to interpretations for which this condition is not met are just not models for that theory.

There are at least the following differences:

(1) Any relational structure which satisfies 1 and 2 above is a model for a logical formalism, but models in physics are more tightly constrained.
(2) A semantic basis is only a model in physics if it is physically plausible relative to the common ontology of a certain epoch.
    (a) The model must be abstracted from a determinate source.
    (b) The source must be of a type with known entitative systems, as we shall establish in Chapter Five.

4. The 'set theoretic' or 'non-statement' account of models and theories

From the point of view expounded in this book, there is no fundamental distinction between observational and theoretical concepts. Which category a given concept will fall into at any moment in the history of a science depends on historical accident. In our account of science the distinction 'observation/theory' plays no fundamental part. However, the distinction played a very large role in the attempts by the logicists of the 'Vienna' school to give a formal account of science. The positivism which infected their thought meant that the meanings of expressions which were not instantiated observationally posed some sort of problem. The problem had a logical core since the logicist account of theories was based on the ideal of an axiomatic structure, and theoretical terms would surely be characteristic of the axiomatic level of the deductive hierarchy of law statements that constituted the theory. The 'non-statement' account of theories, which, when shorn of its pretentious symbolic garb, is in most respects more or less identical with the naturalistic account, developed out of an attempt by Sneed (1971) to resolve the issue of the status of theoretical concepts in physics. Since we have no place for the distinction we shall merely note Sneed's version of it in passing, and make only the most minimal comments. Our interest is in the question of whether the formal treatment of theories as sets of models has any advantage over the naturalistic treatment from which our semi-formal account is derived.

As formulated by Stegmüller (1979: 41), Sneed's criterion for theoreticity runs as follows: 'quantities or functions whose values cannot be calculated without recourse to a successfully applied theory are theoretical in relation to that theory.' If we need the theory of chemical ions to calculate the value of a transport number in physical chemistry, then the concept 'transport number' is theoretical. Unfortunately the example Stegmüller uses to illustrate the point is badly chosen. He supposes that one would need 'classical mechanics' (though he does not say which version, and that matters!) to give a numerical value to 'mass' and 'force' but would not require it to give a numerical value to 'position'. How 'position' would be measured without recourse to an inertial frame escapes us. So the example is unhappy, but one gets the general idea. However, this old debate is irrelevant for our discussion since we simply do not recognise the observation/theory distinction as having any semantic, ontological or epistemological significance.

The basic idea behind the 'non-statement' account of science is that we could imagine the world to be made up of an indefinite array of systems, each of which could be idealised as a set-theoretic structure. Each system could be presented as a set of elements and relations. Each such idealisation could serve as a model, in the logician's sense, of some abstract mathematical structure. To each abstract structure will correspond a set of idealised systems, the intended applications. A theory, on the non-statement view, consists of just such a structure and its intended applications. It does not consist of a deductive hierarchy of sentences. As Sneed remarks (1974: 253), '... we must begin to look at the phenomena "as if " they were models [in the sense of mathematical logic] for abstract structures' and the steps to achieve this 'already entail a significant amount of idealisation'. Thus far the basic theme of the non-statement account is identical with the naturalistic treatment, but for one important detail. What we have called the 'cognitive object' or 'content of a theory or theory-family' – that is the set of models for the theory – is called the 'theory' by the non-statementists. We think that nothing but confusion can arise from a terminology which tempts a reader to confuse a discourse with its subject matter. We shall retain the ordinary usage of the word 'theory': that it is to be used as a word for a description of some one of the set of models – that is, taken to be the most verisimilitudinous at some moment in its evolution.

We must now briefly set out a formulation of the non-statement view as it is to be found in Stegmüller (1976). We start with a reminder of the new use for the word 'theory'. To avoid misunderstandings we shall henceforth use the expression Sneed-Stegmüller or SS-theory for a mathematical structure (to be referred as MS) and its intended applications (IAs). The non-statement idea can be expressed in terms of three main notions:

(1) The 'matrix' of an SS-theory is the set of entities which may have the structure MS.
(2) The 'frame' of an SS-theory includes the set M of all actual models of MS (in the logician's sense of 'model') together with Mp, the set of all possible models of MS. In addition the frame includes the set of all conceivable applications, Mpp, and a function 'r' which serves to differentiate the set Mpp into two parts, one theoretical and one non-theoretical in Sneed's sense of that highly polymorphous term.
(3) The 'core' of an SS-theory is simply the frame of the theory plus a 'constraint'. A constraint is a function which eliminates

certain intended applications from the set of possible models, essentially those picked out in the frame as theoretical.

If the non-statement view of science had been confined to principles (i) and (ii) above, and care taken not to be misled by its advocates' eccentric use of the word 'theory', there would be little to differentiate it from the naturalistic analysis, even though it is presented at a very high level of generality.

We shall now turn to examine the non-statement view in its full form. There is one obvious advantage, illustrated in a paper by Diedrich (1989). Since it is presented at a very high level of generality it should represent the root ideas in an adequate account of any scientific enterprise. But a high level of generality has certain disadvantages, particularly an inevitable vagueness when one tries to apply it in concrete cases. This is a general problem with the use of formal representations of cognitive practices, for instance the impossibility of representing the various modes of generality expressible in ordinary language in terms of the standard quantifiers of first-order predicate calculus.

A more particular disadvantage of the SS treatment *vis à vis* the naturalistic analysis of model use is the inversion of the actual order of genesis of physical theories. In the SS treatment the mathematical structure is among the givens and the problem, if we may put it this way, is to find the best model. But in real science the model or models are in hand and the problem is to find the best mathematical structure to capture their main structural features. Connected with this weakness is the inability of the SS treatment to express the way that sets of models for theories (in the traditional sense) are ordered. There is nothing in the SS view which would tell us that van der Waal's model for the gas laws is more sophisticated than that of Amagat. Connected again to both of these shortcomings is the failure of the treatment to express the dialectic interaction between models and mathematical structures which is the heart of the process of theory development. Usually, though not always, theoretical innovation and/or experimental discoveries pre-exist transformations in the mathematical structure which is altered to accommodate them. To our way of thinking these disparities and lacunae are serious disadvantages in a program which purports to capture the essence of theorising in the physical sciences.

But there is a much more serious problem with the SS-treatment. It seems quite clear that it presupposes a covert positivism. It purports to give a formal account of the empirical content of theories in physics. So does our treatment in terms of type-hierarchies. But there the resemblance ends. We can bring out the difficulty by focusing on the ontological implications of Stegmüller's actual formulation of the SS point of view. He refers in many places to 'classical mechanics'. There is, as anyone who has taught physics knows, no such thing, at the level of physical theory. There are at least the Newtonian, the Hamiltonian and the Hertzian formulations of a genus of theories we could loosely call 'classical mechanics'. These formulations are not notational variants of some common theory. They are ontologically quite distinct. The Newtonian version is based on an ontology of forces, atoms and a (notorious) container version of the absolutist view of space and time. The Hamiltonian version is based on an energeticist ontology, while the Hertzian way of formulating mechanics makes no use of energy or force, and is a pure mechanics of mass-points. And there are other versions too. For us this means that the three versions are different theories and in particular they must have different empirical content. How could they be elided as one theory (in the SS sense) with the same empirical content, as Stegmüller and Sneed seem to imply in their use of the expression 'classical mechanics' as if it denoted one theory? Seemingly only under positivism. Each theory generates the same sets of numbers representing the results of actual or *Gedanken* experiments in mechanics, though by very different routes. Sneed's remark about 'phenomena', which we have already quoted, leads us to think that there is indeed a covert positivism embedded in the SS point of view. We would like to take the greatest possible distance from the idea that the empirical content of a theory is to be confined to what is non-theoretical either in Sneed's sense or in the observation limit sense of the older positivists. In our view Sneed's distinction between theoretical and non-theoretical qualities and functions (to use Stegmüller's phrase) is defective. It is no more sustainable in actual applications than was the logical positivist distinction based upon their meaning criterion. If the 'ontologically reductive' aspect we have detected is indeed a feature of this point of view, it accounts for the attraction the non-statement view has had for such quasi-positivists as van Fraasen. In the end all that the SS view amounts to is a high-tec version of the old point that a physical theory and the world meet in isomorphisms between sets of numbers, those generated by the relevant apparatus and those generated by the theory. In this banal observation we note the crucial importance of mappings between mathematical structures and their models, as intended applications.

5. *Icon* and *Bild*: Hertz's account of mechanics

The double interpretation of certain cognitive objects used by physicists, as a formal treatment of the content of physical theory, is by no means original to the present generation of philosophers of science. It was the central insight of Hertz's philosophy of physics and descended directly to the 'picture theory' of Wittgenstein's *Tractatus*. 'We form for ourselves images (*Bilder*) or symbols of external objects; and the form which we give them is such that the necessary consequents of the images in thought are always necessary consequents in nature of the things pictured' (Hertz, 1894: 1). According to Hertz such 'images' must be permissible, appropriate and correct. That an image is permissible 'is given by the nature of our mind'; that image is the more appropriate which 'pictures more of the essential relations of external things'; an image is incorrect if 'its essential relations contradict the relations of external things' (Hertz, 1894: 2).

What exactly does Hertz mean by an 'image'? Clearly an important constraint on a scientific image is the set of laws governing the behaviour of phenomena, and the hypotheses introducing the unobservable entities necessary to complete the image given empirically, together with what Hertz calls the 'normal connections' of things (Hertz, 1894: 28). What could a row of symbols, a formula, and the motion of a body relative to some frame of reference have in common so that the former could be an image of the latter? Hertz seems to have had in mind a formal correspondence, some kind of isomorphism of structure. Such an isomorphism would need to be mediated somehow. One possibility is that a formula is a *Bild* of a physical process if there is a one-to-one correspondence between the set of consequents of applying the formula in some specified conditions, an ordered sequence of numbers, for instance, and the set of consequents of running the process in some apparatus yielding another set of numbers, the numerical measures of the successive states of that physical system while the process is running. In this way the formula '$s = ut + 1/2gt^2$' could be an image of the falling of a weight in an Atwood's machine.

We shall retain the German word '*Bild*' for this very abstract sense of picture in which the picture-world relation is mediated by a formal mapping between ordered sets of numbers. We could use the Greek word '*icon*' for the more concrete pictures that are created by the kind of modelling we have described in Chapter Three. By extending the concept of 'picture' in this way we too can offer a general account of theorising without abandoning the insights into detail that we derived from the naturalistic approach. Just as the ionic theory of chemical reactions maps phenomena onto states of affairs specified in a common ontology (irrespective of any contingent constraints on observability), so theories like Galilean kinematics, special relativity and Newtonian dynamics also function as just such maps. The sparse conceptual structure of the various forms of mechanics is the result of the collapse of some of the distinctions drawn in our general account of theorising into one another. In the naturalistic account we identified two 'regions' or submodels of the basic iconic model on which a theory is dependent. There was a descriptive model abstracted from observed phenomena. And there was the explanatory model by which a physicist could anticipate some form of human contact with an as yet untouched realm of physical beings. In classical kinematics and in special relativity nothing is hidden. Descriptive model and explanatory model collapse into one another, or to put it another way there are no differentiable regions in the general models or *Bilder* of kinematic phenomena constituted by the formulae of classical kinematics or special relativity. In the descriptive account we distinguished between statements describing iconic models and those models. In the Hertzian treatment even that distinction collapses, since the formulae which serve as the sentences with which kinematic statements can be made are also constitutive of the model. The same collapse is to be seen in the various versions of classical dynamics. Though each draws on a different common ontology, in the Hertzian interpretation the set of formulae is the model, and the theory-to-world mediation by isomorphic sets of numbers is just the same.

There is a danger for philosophy in using mechanics as the prime example of a physical theory. The textbook presentation of a system of mechanical laws as a deductively organised ordered set of formulae looks very much like an example of the Cartesian or deductive-nomological account of physical theory. Hertz's treatment of theories in physics as abstract *Bilder* permits a view of the structure of many important physical theories as collapsed versions of the structure revealed in the general naturalistic analysis of theorising.

6. Summary

(1) In general a model is related to its description 'internally'. An entitative interpreting domain which is to serve as a semantic basis for a formal structure is a model for a theory only if the sentences created by interpreting the formulae of the theory by that semantic basis can be used to make true statements about the domain. The dynamics of theory development is largely controlled by this imperative. Theory and model are continuously mutually adjusted, in so far as that is possible.

(2) However, in physics models are subject to an ontological constraint. They are related to the states of affairs they purport to represent 'externally'. Issues of faithfulness and degree of resemblance to their external correlates can be raised.

(3) In the naturalistic analysis of model use we see that models are created for practical purposes and then described in a theoretical discourse, which comes, so to say, already interpreted. The main constraint is physical plausibility.

(4) In the logical analysis of model use we see that models are introduced to interpret a pre-existing abstract formalism. Models in this context are constrained only by the internal requirement of a common formal structure. In real science models are types in a type-hierarchy.

CHAPTER FIVE

The Type-hierarchy Approach to Models

1. The traditional account of models

According to Campbell (1957), a theory must consist of *four* elements: a formal deductive system of axioms and theorems, a dictionary mapping terms of the formal system into experimental terms, experimental laws, *and* analogy. However, Campbell's approach to models and analogies is 'bottom up', that is, models are generated by directly comparing two systems, based on an unanalysed notion of bare similarity. These similarity comparisons are used to generate analogical relationships between the model and unknown system, and they are the means by which the properties of the former are transferred to the latter. Since Campbell's interpretation of models and analogies is still within the paradigm of the positivist view of theories, the addition of analogy will consist of adding a set of propositions asserting similarities to the traditional structure.

We think that this bottom-up approach to analogies is responsible for well-known problems associated with models. We will advocate that the traditional approach be replaced by a 'top-down' analysis of models and their place in theories, where theories are not thought of in terms of the hypothetico-deductive structure. Instead of analysing theories as sets of propositions with additional similarity propositions tacked on, theories are thought of as essentially involving chunks of type-hierarchies as they were characterised in the Chapter Two. We think that by portraying theories and analogies as sets of propositions Campbell is playing into the hands of the formalists.

2. Problems with the traditional approach to models and analogies

a. The alleged dispensability of models

One of the most hotly debated issues in the philosophy of science concerns the dispensability of models in scientific theories. One school of thought, that of Campbell and Hesse, maintains that the use of models is the essence of scientific theorising, that without them we could never achieve an understanding of phenomena. On the other hand, philosophers of the logicist persuasion, such as Duhem and Hempel, have maintained that models are simply picturing devices, having only pragmatic value. According to the logicist school, models are far from being essential to theory. They claim that once models have been used as psychological devices to conceptualise a hypothesis, the logical syntax of the theory takes over and the model itself can be discarded. Since the D-N version of a scientific theory is a formal one that contains laws of nature and a logical structure which can entail descriptions of the phenomena in question by deduction from descriptions of the initial conditions, once a theory is developed the laws will entirely explain the phenomena and the model becomes superfluous. The formalist cannot conceive of a theory without the formal structure of axioms, dictionaries and laws, these elements are part of the very mechanism of deduction, but it is easy to conceive of a theory without the additional set of similarity assertions. Thus models are seen as just pragmatic devices which can be of use in developing the correct logical structure but are in no way necessary for the final explanatory theory.

On the other side of the debate are those who argue that models are the very essence of scientific theories, that these models play a much greater role in science than merely pragmatic aids for the deduction of predictions. Not only does the interpretation of the theory via a model give us greater explanatory power – since formal representations of laws are not especially illuminating – but the use of models also accounts for the *dynamic nature* of theories. Theories are generative in a way that fixed axioms are not. In the practice of science a theory is never a static and isolated device; rather, theories are continu-

ously being revised and extended to fit new phenomena. If a
theory is merely a formal or mathematical entity, any such
extensions must be arbitrary. It is the structure and possibilities
contained in the model that guides and unifies extensions of a
scientific theory. Thus models are able to approximate the world
in a way that formal axioms cannot, which is one reason why
Campbell, Hesse, Harré, Aronson, Giere and other proponents
of models think that theories are more than mere sets of propositions.

However, despite the debate, and despite the fact that the
logicist view of scientific theories has generally been rejected, it
is still unclear exactly *why* models play an indispensable role:
what is it about models that cannot be captured formally? It
must be more than just that they serve as the basis for a set of
similarity assertions. The problem is that once a model is developed and clearly articulated, the formalist can always claim that
the role of the model can be reduced to just such a set of formal
propositions. The initial conditions and the laws can all be
symbolised and the predictions that the model originally generated will now directly fall out of this formal structure by deduction. In order to block this move by the formalist, the proponent
of models must demonstrate that there are aspects of scientific
theories and models which are not and cannot be captured by a
corresponding set of propositions.

b. The problem of filtering positive from negative analogies

One of the basic dilemmas of modelling is that the model must
always have areas which do not correspond to the system being
modelled. The areas that do correspond are the *positive* analogies and the areas that do not comprise the negative and neutral
analogies. James Gleick explains the problem as follows:

> The choice is always the same. You can make your model more
> complex and more faithful to reality, or you can make it simpler
> and easier to handle. Only the most naive scientist believes that
> the perfect model is one that perfectly represents reality. Such a
> model would have the same drawbacks as a map as large and
> detailed as the city it represents, a map depicting every park,
> every street, every building, every tree, every pothole, every
> inhabitant, and every map. Were such a map possible, its speci-
> ficity would defeat its purpose: to generalise and abstract. Map-

makers highlight such features as their clients choose. Whatever their purpose, maps and models must simplify as much as they mimic the world. (1987, pp. 278-9)

Thus any model must be a *partial* mapping between the model and the system modelled; otherwise we merely have an uninteresting duplication of the system or phenomena, not an explanatory model. However, if the model is a partial mapping, what determines which parts are mapped and which are not?

The traditional comparison view of models is beset with this age-old problem of filtering positive from negative analogies in a non *ad hoc* way. If *A* is a theoretical model for some real system *B*, then the positive analogy is those properties or respects in which *A* and *B* are similar. The negative analogy consists of those respects in which *A* and *B* are different, and the neutral analogy consists of those properties or respects which either have no corresponding map to the other or which have not yet been explored. The comparison view lines up and compares these properties for similarity and difference, and the amount of similarity is simply a matter of counting.

As compelling as the traditional analysis is, it contains a central flaw: it cannot explain how the selection of properties which are to be taken as the significant similarities is determined. When the sets of properties of the theoretical model and the real world entity are enumerated and lined up for comparison, what determines the mapping? Imagine for example the properties of the solar system (the model) and that of the atom (the entity being modelled). Some similarities seem obvious: entities which have an elliptical orbit (planets/electrons) around a central object (sun/nucleus). But why is this an obvious mapping? Why do we map only *some* of the physical and structural features which are present while ignoring others? Clearly some properties are more important or *salient* than others for the model; how are these determined? Why don't we consider that electrons may have an analogy with moons, craters or an atmosphere; or that the nucleus may have a gaseous and turbulent structure? How do we know, for example, that mass should map onto charge and not weight?

The comparison view provides us with no way to filter the positive from the negative analogies because simply comparing the properties of the two systems in isolation is not enough;

analogical reasoning cannot occur in a vacuum. When we carefully consider the properties of the solar system and the atom,
the mapping of the comparison view is clearly seen as arbitrary,
and the filtering of the positive from the negative aspects will,
by necessity, be *ad hoc*.

c. The problem of trivial and non-trivial analogies

Another problem that arises from the traditional view of models
is that structural isomorphism is not a powerful enough relation
to account for the difference between trivial and non-trivial
models. If the only criterion for one system to model another is
comparing the two systems for similarity, i.e. locating an isomorphism between them, then there will be an endless number of
systems that exhibit the requisite mapping. However, most of
these isomorphisms will have no explanatory power when used
as a model for the unknown system. For example, a racing car
driving on an elliptical track around a house and a planet
orbiting the sun may both be similar to the atom with respect to
the shape of motion, and the degree of such a similarity may be
equally close for the two systems; but we still want to say that
the solar system provides us with a better explanatory model of
the atom than the racing car system.

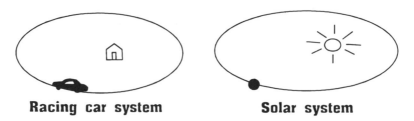

Racing car system   **Solar system**

Figure 5.1. Racing car and solar system models

Using only the criterion of structural isomorphism to determine
a model, we have no grounds to eliminate trivial models like that
of the racing car and the house. Why is the solar system a good
model for explaining the atom and the racing car a feeble one?
Both models can claim the virtue of similarity. The racing car
maps to an electron and the house in the centre of the track maps
to the nucleus and the motion of the car corresponds to the

elliptical motion of an electron. By using only bare or un-weighted similarity in comparisons of sets of properties, the comparison view cannot distinguish between interesting and trivial models, nor can it determine relevant or salient similarities from empty ones. In the end, the comparison view is forced to resolve the mapping between a system and its model *ad hoc*: it is those mapping which work, and those which have the power to explain: that is, that are taken to be significant.

These shortcomings of the comparison view of analogy and models have not gone unnoticed. (See Harré, 1986 and Wylie, 1988). This weakness must be eliminated in some principled way, since critics are only too ready to draw the conclusion that these problems show either that analogical reasoning is inherently unreliable and should not be used in science or that analogical inference should be assimilated into an inference which is on firmer ground. We shall argue that both of these responses are mistaken. Instead of rejecting models wholesale what is needed is a new conception of similarity, salience and the modelling relation. Elsewhere we have offered an alternative analysis of the salience criterion (Harré, 1986; Way, 1991) and we have argued that what is important in a model is dependent upon the *ontological* assumptions which give rise to natural kind constraints. It is this line which we will develop here. By changing our view of scientific models and by introducing the notion of weighted similarity we can deal with the problems of positive and negative analogies in a non-arbitrary way.

d. Giere's approach and the problem of taking bare similarity as the basic unanalysed relation

A recent view which holds models to be indispensable to scientific theories is Giere's theory of approximation. Giere denies that theories are sets of propositions; rather, he proposes, as many before him have held, that theories are families of models, models which are related by *similarity* to each other and to the real world. His purpose in developing such an approach is to come up with an account of scientific progress without using what he calls 'a bastard semantical relationship – approximate truth' (1988: 106). His project is identical with ours. Our main interest here is in Giere's characterisation of scientific models. We will not go into his theory of approximation in detail in this chapter.

Giere considers models to be *abstract entities* which scientists use to represent the world. A scientific theory consists of a cluster or family of these models. These abstract entities have no reality beyond that given to them by the community of scientists but they are to be considered *objects* not linguistic or logical entities. Furthermore, Giere claims that the relationship between these abstract entities and the real world is not that of truth but of similarity. Similarity is also the relationship *between* the models in a family or cluster.

> The relationship that does the heavy representational work is not one of truth between a linguistic entity and a real object, but of similarity between two objects, one abstract and one real. From this point of view the difficulties with the standard view arise because it tries to forge a direct semantic link between the statements characterising the model and the world – thus eliminating the role of models altogether. (1988: 82)

According to Giere, scientific models cannot be viewed as sets of propositions because the relationship connecting sets of propositions to the world is *linguistic*, while the relationship necessary to explain how theoretical models are tied to the world is similarity. By replacing truth and reference with similarity, Giere plans to bypass the problems of realism and truth.

The question of whether Giere has answered the formalists by finding an aspect of models which cannot be captured by sets of propositions depends crucially upon his notion of the relation of similarity. In his theory, the similarity relation is used not only to interlink families of models but also to explicate the relation between each model and the world. Thus, because of Giere's heavy reliance on the notion of similarity, his theory can only be considered as good as his analysis of this relation. Unfortunately, Giere treats similarity as a logically primitive or basic unanalysed notion in his system, and so no such analysis is forthcoming. How the similarity relation is unpacked will greatly affect the implications and interpretation of his theory.

For example, Giere must address the issue of what properties the similarity relation possesses: is it symmetric, transitive, reflexive? If similarity is defined to be a symmetric or transitive relation, as many people believe, then, on Giere's theory, there would be no motivation for saying that any model is better than any other at representing the phenomena, since each model is related to a family of others by similarity. Yet this is clearly not the case. Giere's notion of similarity is not rich enough to give us a ranking of models in terms of which are the better approximations. But this was to be the main objective of his analysis.

In order for him to rank models in terms of the relation of 'better approximation', he must account for how some things can be *more* similar than others, and explicate what determines the amount and degree of similarity. The notion of similarity is doing too much of the work in Giere's theory; and similarity is too complex and difficult a notion to leave as an unanalysed primitive. As Searle has observed concerning the use of similarity for explicating metaphor:

> Similarity is a vacuous predicate; and any two things are similar in some respect or other. Saying that the metaphorical '*S* is *P*' implies the literal '*S* is like *P*' does not solve our problem. It only pushes it back a step. The problem of understanding literal similes with the respect of the similarity left unspecified is only a part of the problem of understanding metaphor. How are we supposed to know, for example, that the utterance 'Juliet is the sun' does not mean 'Juliet is for the most part gaseous,' or 'Juliet is 90 million miles from the earth,' both of which properties are salient and well-known features of the sun. (Searle, 1979: 106)

Giere is sensitive to the problems inherent in relying on the bare similarity relation alone. He states that assertions of similarity must always be restricted to a particular set of *respects* and *degrees*:

> But since anything is similar to anything else in some way or other, the claim of similarity must be limited (at least implicitly) to a specified set of respects and degrees. (p. 93)

Unfortunately Giere does not explain how these respects and degrees are to be determined when using a scientific model. Furthermore similarity simply with respect to a property and in terms of so many degrees will still not provide us with enough differentiation to say that one model is more similar to a target system than another. Once again, the model of the racing car and that of the solar system may share the same degree of similarity with the atom. But we still want to say that the solar system provides us with a better model for the atom than the racing car system. Giere is really using a *comparison* view of models and analogy. He simply enumerates the properties which the model and the system being modelled possess, and compares them for similarity. The fault does not lie so much with Giere's analysis of approximation as it does with the traditional approach to the nature of models and analogies in the philosophy of science. The problems of analogical reasoning, metaphor and scientific models are intimately related. We will see in the next section that the problems that plague the traditional approach to models have a close parallel in the dispute about the relative status of literal and metaphoric language.

3. The traditional approach to literal and metaphorical language

The tradition in philosophy of language and science is that language is intrinsically literal in nature. Literal meaning is considered to be the normal and standard use of words, and it is the meaning that words possess independently of when and how they are used. These meanings are considered to be objective and correspond with various aspects of the world. Metaphor, on the other hand, involves using words in ways that do not agree with their normal and standard usage; hence, the meaning is highly ambiguous and contextual. Metaphorical utterances frequently do not directly correspond with entities and events in the world: that is, metaphoric statements are often literally false. Thus metaphor and other forms of non-literal speech are considered to be *deviant* forms of language that are dependent on, and hence reducible to, the standard literal form. According to this picture, figurative language is 'emotional' and non-descriptive. In order for language to be purely scientific, the meaning of any meta-phorical statement should be reduced to a literal paraphrase or statements of direct comparison. The proper language for science and other serious discourse is literal language with its Tarskian correspondence for truth conditions.

The most popular reductionist theory of metaphor is that of

the comparison view: metaphor is really an elliptical form of simile or literal analogy. For example, when we say 'Bruce is a bear', the comparison view holds that we are really saying that Bruce is *like* a bear in certain respects but these similarities are not explicitly spelled out. Obviously, Bruce is not literally a bear; the metaphor is merely pointing out properties that they both have in common. However, their respective sets of properties cannot be identical: bears are large, fur-covered creatures known for their dangerous temper when disturbed, while Bruce may be large for a man but he is small for a bear; and he may be grumpy and ill-tempered but he is not likely to kill if disturbed. The comparison between properties is not based on identity but involves similarity. The meaning of the metaphorical statement, then, is a set of literal statements of similarity comparisons between the properties of bears and the properties possessed by Bruce. Since the similarity relations between features are assumed to exist independently of the objects being compared, the literal analogy follows naturally from the explicit comparison.

We can see that the above account of the meaning of metaphorical statements in terms of literal statements of similarity directly parallels the treatment of analogy in traditional accounts of theories. Just as models are reduced to propositions expressing similarity in the logicist view so metaphors are reduced to literal statements of explicit comparison. Furthermore all the problems that plague the Campbellian account of models have their counterparts in the comparison view of metaphor. If models are merely sets of similarity propositions added on to the formal structure of a theory, then they do not seem to be an indispensable part of explanatory theories. Likewise if metaphorical statements are completely equivalent to literal speech, then they have no intrinsic value and add only stylistic rather than substantive quality to speech. As the above Searle quotation shows, the comparison view of metaphor has the same problem of principled filtering of positive from negative analogies. Likewise in the example of Bruce and bears the theory cannot explain why size and temperament are the positive analogies, while fur, claws, fishing, cave-dwelling and hibernation are part of the negative.

Finally, both the comparison view of metaphor and the traditional view of models treat similarity as primitive and unproblematic. This is a mistake. As we saw in Chapter Two, similarity is not a constant and immutable relation between two entities or concepts, but its content varies widely depending on context and our understanding of the world (recall the difference in perceived similarity between the colours white and grey with respect to clouds and hair). Thus the content of a particular similarity relation cannot be characterised in terms of the number of match-ups between individual features but is dynamically determined for each comparison by the organisation of our concepts and the content of our theories about the world. In fact, as Max Black (1962: 37) has suggested, it appears that metaphor *creates* the similarity rather than being dependent on some similarity antecedently existing.

However, if similarity is itself complex and dependent upon other cognitive mechanisms, as we claim, then it cannot be used as a primitive notion in reducing metaphor, models and analogies to literal language. Furthermore there has been a great deal of work recently on re-evaluating logic-based views of language, in particular, a re-evaluation of the role that metaphor and other figurative speech plays in language. First of all the analysis of scientific language assumed by the logicist philosophers of science is not in accordance with actual scientific practice. Metaphors abound in all areas of human endeavour, including science and others once thought to be the epitome of literal logical language. Models and metaphors are now seen as central to language and reasoning, and some even argue that all meaning is essentially metaphorical. However, such a radical change cannot be made in isolation; rather it calls for a revision of our theories of language, truth and meaning. As Mary Hesse (1988: 320) asks, 'How are we to interpret the notions of truth and reference within a scientific language pervaded by metaphor, and in theories based on analogical models?' We address some of these issues in the next section. How truth is interpreted in terms of a scientific language pervaded by metaphor is taken up in Chapter Six.

4. Type-hierarchies depict literal and metaphorical language

Although metaphorical language has a long history of being viewed as an aberrant and misleading form of speech, it was not until the seventeenth century that the literal-truth paradigm became the accepted ideal of language. The motivation for this view was the desire to model speech and argumentation upon the elegance and simplicity of mathematics and geometry. For the rationalist and empiricist philosophers of the time, the ideal rational language was that of science: scientific experience and knowledge was taken to be the model for all human experience and knowledge.

However, the logicist approach to science and language has been fraught with difficulties, and many philosophers of science now doubt that scientific theories can be adequately analysed as deductively organised sets of propositions. Instead theories are better characterised as involving models or families of models. But since the literal paradigm of language has remained entrenched in standard analytical philosophy, giving an account of scientific theories in terms of models has proved to be problematic. The above difficulties in the analysis of models and metaphors arise directly from the mistaken belief that literal, propositional language is and should be the basis for serious or scientific language. The role of models, analogies and metaphors in everyday life as well as in science has begun to be recognised to such an extent that many now claim that metaphor is fundamental to all meaning. Mary Hesse (1993: 56), for example, claims that 'metaphor properly understood has logical priority over the literal, and hence that natural language is fundamentally metaphorical, with the "literal" occurring as a kind of limiting case'.

Many philosophers fear that if we reject the view that scientific theories can be characterised as sets of propositions and replace the literal-truth paradigm with the holistic and context-dependent paradigm of metaphorical language, we will lose all hope of a clear and formal treatment of language and scientific theories. However, recent developments in artificial intelligence (AI) have produced a new spectrum of tools for analysing, clarifying and exploring traditional theories of meaning and language. Computational models are excellent tools for testing the power and scope of a theory, and AI models have graphically demonstrated that there are serious problems with a logic-based view of language. What is needed is a new approach to language, one which comes closer to capturing the flexibility and range of natural language without losing the explication of a formalisation (Way, 1991). Mary Hesse (1988: 317) recognises the need for this approach in the following passage:

> Metaphorical meaning and analogical reasoning have now become issues within AI in terms of programs for problem solving. Part of the reason for this has been the sterility of attempts within logic and linguistics to account for the cognitive processes that are fundamentally analogical rather than deductive.

Programs in AI can be seen as an embodiment of a theory in computational form; however, the rigorous requirements of implementing a theory in a programming language will clarify implicit assumptions and vague notions and, in so doing, reveal problems which had not previously been considered. Thus in using computational models we can answer the formalist by providing theories which are as precise as the predicate calculus but which are cognitive rather than propositional in nature (Way, 1991: 51).

We are now in a position to use the ideas and concepts from artificial intelligence to explicate an alternative, knowledge-intensive account of models, language and metaphor. We will use the material developed in Chapter Two on the notion of type-hierarchies and the ordering of natural kinds to depict the mechanism underlying both literal and figurative speech. Here we have a means of clearly and unambiguously expressing the global nature of similarity and meaning, since the structure of the type-hierarchy incorporates our understandings of the complex interrelations among properties and kinds. The structure of this type-hierarchy carries the burden of making the distinction between literal and figurative language clear. According to this view of the nature of language, literal and figurative language are associated with different aspects of a type-hierarchy (Way, 1991).

Unlike Hesse's above proposal, we do not hold that metaphor

has logical priority over the literal, nor do we agree with Lakoff and Johnson (1980) that the literal/metaphorical distinction is vacuous. However, we do not adhere to the traditional view of literal language as objective, context-independent and stable. Nor, as we shall see in Chapter Six, do we keep with the traditional Tarskian analysis of truth and verisimilitude. Rather we hold that both literal and metaphorical language are highly context-dependent, subject to meaning shifts and a result of similar cognitive mechanisms. In other words, literal and figurative language are considered to be on a par.

The role that context plays in metaphor can be represented as a set of *masks* which change the view of the semantic hierarchy. Whether a statement is literal, metaphorical or figurative depends upon what mask comes into play and what connections in the hierarchy are hidden or exposed by it. Metaphor, then, takes place by establishing new semantic linkages as a result of coarse-grained masking. What we have, here, is a 'neutral' type-hierarchy that exhibits all possible links between type nodes (see Figure 5.2).

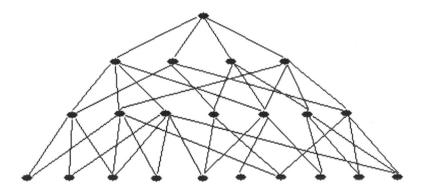

Figure 5.2. Original type-hierarchy

When a masking operation occurs, certain links in the hierarchy are blocked out. Different masks come into play, depending on whether the speech act is figurative or literal; hence different links are blocked out and different hierarchies result from these masking operations (Figure 5.3) (Way, 1991: 127-8). Notice that in the case of metaphor, there are more links among semantic domains. This is why the metaphor mask is coarse-grained.

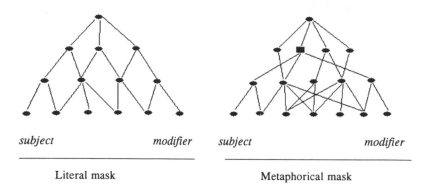

Literal mask   Metaphorical mask

Figure 5.3. Masked hierarchies

The result of the masking is that the tenor or subject of the metaphor is redescribed in terms of the new hierarchy brought into play by the ontology of the vehicle or modifier. And that, according to our view, is what metaphor is: the redescription of one domain in terms of the generated hierarchy and the associated beliefs from another. Since these hierarchies reflect our view of the world, we are redescribing the subject in terms of a new and different view of the world. In fact figurative language can be viewed as a result of intentionally 'juggling' the links of a type-hierarchy in order to explore possibilities or extend the meaning of our concepts (Way, 1991). But then is not this what models are all about?

What then is a 'literal' use of words, according to this theory of language? 'Literal' partially denotes the presently accepted classification of natural kinds and species. Literal speech occurs when the speaker succeeds in communicating to the listener that aspect of a type-hierarchy which can be identified with what we ordinarily consider to be the classification of natural kinds and species. But this means that such a view of language has the literal-figurative contrast already built-in, simply because literal and figurative contexts cannot mask out the very same aspect of a type-hierarchy. Thus, to say that all uses of language are metaphorical would amount to saying that there are no contextual operations on a type-hierarchy that yield connections which reflect the actual way we classify natural kinds and species of things; but this is clearly not the case.

According to the above outlined theory, it is not the inherent structure of the written or spoken word that determines whether an expression is literal or figurative but that aspect of the hierarchy which is invoked by the context behind a particular use of language. This view places figurative use of language on an equal footing with literal as *complementary* aspects of the same type-hierarchy. Both literal and metaphorical language are now viewed as context dependent, and it is impossible to reduce the figurative to the literal and *vice versa*. This theory can now make perfectly good sense of how metaphor can permeate language in that non-standard classifications are always available to the language user; yet, this fact is explained in such a way as to preserve the literal-figurative distinction (Way, 1991).

Finally, there is another, very important feature of the literal-figurative distinction which any theory must take into account: the boundary of what is literal and figurative is constantly shifting; we all know that today's metaphor may be literal tomorrow and *vice versa*. Figurative uses of language may, in time, turn out to be accepted by the community of speakers as truth-bearing and new connections may be forged between old concepts in order to fill in 'gaps' in language and in our conceptual repertoire. Thus connections between concepts that were originally thought to be unorthodox or even bizarre may actually be found to be correct. We have seen this happen so often with the advent of scientific metaphors. Likewise, especially in science, theories that were accepted as the literal truth ended up being 'demoted' to the realm of convenient metaphors: for example, the fluid theory of gases and the ether as a medium for electromagnetic radiation. Thus, if we are going to use the notion of a type-hierarchy to explain literal and figurative uses of language, it will have to be a *dynamic* type-hierarchy, where the links between types are constantly shifting over time. In the next section we will see how the formalism of a type-hierarchy and the mechanisms of metaphor can give us a sounder basis for explicating scientific models and analogies.

5. Contrasting the type-hierarchy approach to models with the comparison view

Giere is correct to hold that scientific theories are more than just a series of propositions, but he does not realise that theories are also more than just descriptions of a family of models; that in fact models are 'just the tip of the iceberg'. Scientific theories are metaphysical devices for expressing the ontology of our world. The nature of an explanation is relativised to the kinds of entities, properties and interactions named by the theory, and the kinds of predictions it can make will be dependent upon the ontology it presupposes.

Thus, even though we agree with many aspects of Giere's theory and believe he is on the right track to talk about theories in terms of families of models, unless he is able to unpack the similarity relation his theory will be beset with difficulties. Furthermore, once the similarity relation is analysed, Giere may find that instead of bypassing the troublesome questions of truth and realism he has unknowingly incorporated them at the most basic level of his treatment of models (see Aronson, 1991). This point will be elaborated in Chapter Six.

A famous alternative to the traditional comparison approach to models, analogy and metaphor is Max Black's *interaction view*. Black (1979) has a more holistic view of the process of metaphor, a view which includes the interaction of entire domains or, as he calls them, 'systems of commonplaces' or 'implication-complex' associated with the terms. Black sees metaphor as filtering one term through another in such a way that certain properties are organised and highlighted, while others are hidden. One particularly suggestive aspect of Black's theory *vis à vis* comparing lists of properties is that metaphor actually *creates* the similarity between terms, rather than capitalising on any which exists previously. This view of metaphor has much to offer any analysis of scientific models, and can reveal how we are to replace the primacy of the literal with the holistic and context-dependent paradigm of metaphorical language.

I am now impressed, as I was insufficiently so when composing *Metaphor*, by the tight connections between the notions of models and metaphors. Every implication-complex supported by a metaphor's secondary subject, I now think, is a *model* of the ascriptions imputed to the primary subject: every metaphor is the tip of a submerged model (Max Black, 1979: 31).

However, Black's approach has been criticised for, among other things, being vague and metaphorical. It is not at all clear how the interaction or filtering is to occur, nor how similarity can be created where none was seen to exist before. In order to take advantage of Black's insights on models and metaphor they have to be made more precise through the tools and techniques in AI and the formalism of a type-hierarchy.

Type-hierarchies give us a powerful means to represent the ordering of natural kinds in a scientific theory in a non propositional way. The inheritance relation determines the application of meta-properties and general laws to particular instances. The structure and ordering of such a hierarchy represent our best metaphysical models of the world. They are based upon empirical evidence and experimentation. It is our contention that only within the context of such an ontological ordering can the mapping of scientific analogy make sense.

Thus we propose an alternative to the comparison view of models and analogy, using Black's intuitions and the formalisms of type-hierarchies for the ordering of natural kinds. This approach can solve the problem of filtering positive from negative analogies in an non-arbitrary way. When we unpack the notion of similarity we will see that, with this analysis, similarity is not a primitive but a *derived* relation. Similarity is a complex, often non-symmetrical relationship, a relationship whose strength is highly dependent on *which* properties the model system and the real system have in common and how these properties are related to one another in terms of a concept of *specificity*. As we have argued (Harré, 1986), we will consider a theory to be based on a taxonomy of natural kinds, a kind of ontological zoo. But we need to add that these natural kinds are ordered according to levels of specificity (Way, 1991). Instead of bare similarity, our primitive relation will be that between a natural kind and a higher-order kind, as it was depicted in Chapter Two. It is the structure of these higher-order relations which determine the relevant or salient properties to use in a comparison between a system and its model: two things are similar in that they are subtypes of the same supertype(s). In Chapter Six we will develop a similarity measure based on Tversky's (1977, 1987) formula that is a function of common and differing supertypes.

Naturally, the way things fall under types will be different with respect to different theories. Thus the question of what is similar to what and in which respects is meaningful only relative to some type-hierarchy. In any system some supertypes will be more important or *salient* than others. The similarity mapping is dependent upon the topology of the hierarchy, and the content and structure of the hierarchy in turn is dependent on an understanding of the world. This understanding includes purposes, the context of the comparison and the subject matter under consideration. It is these factors which determine the importance or rankings of supertypes. Rankings will vary with different theories, purposes, taxonomies and language games. For instance, if we are interested in the fundamental nature of the atom, we may rank the supertype of 'complex systems' as lower in importance than that of 'physical system' when making a comparison with another fundamental entity or system. What the rankings are in a particular instance is an empirical matter that depends upon human intentions and purposes and the structure and order of one's theories. This will be spelled out in more detail in Chapter Six.

Thus a judgment of similarity is not based on a simple comparison of properties but rather a complex concept with an internal structure that goes beyond the logic of a simple predicate. What system can be a good model for another depends upon the overall topographical structure of our metaphysical models of the world. It is this added dimension which Giere's account (and our earlier account) misses. Giere's view takes only the bottom-most slice of this ordering of natural kinds and places the entire burden of similarity comparisons on the local links between this bottom-most layer. However, as we saw above, comparisons between isolated properties of systems are not rich enough to give us non-arbitrary similarity mappings. Unlike the comparison approach, our view of similarity is deeper, going beyond mere appearances, which is the whole point of models in the first place. Analogies must exist in the wider context of a model. In this way, the dependency of models on similarity is reversed. Instead of basing the choice of an explanatory model on prior similarities by making direct comparisons between the known and unknown systems, the similarity comparison and choice of modelling system is *generated* by the supertypes in common between the two systems in the hierarchy. The similarities between them depend upon the model chosen and the properties both inherit from their supertypes. So, rather than using the existence of some structural isomorphism between two systems to determine a model, it is the structure and inheritance relation in the hierarchy that controls the choice of a good model. By using type-hierarchies to represent the structure and ordering of the ontological zoo, we can restore the complexity which underlies the generative mapping of models and analogies and we can reveal how the global, context-dependent nature of metaphor can be incorporated into the very heart of scientific theories.

6. Analogies reconceived

If we return to the example of using the solar system to model the atom, we can illustrate how the positive and negative aspects of an analogy are filtered out. Instead of simply listing and comparing the properties of the atom and the solar system at the bottom-most level, we use the entire structure of the type-hierarchy to propose that the atom may fit into our ontological scheme under the same supertypes as that of the solar system. This means that the atom must inherit all the meta-properties that a solar system can inherit. Of course, when attempting to explain an unknown system in terms of a known system, we may try many different locations in our ontological scheme (or type-hierarchy). At one time it was suggested that the structure of the atom might best resemble that of plum pudding – a sponge-like solid with denser matter (raisins) scattered throughout. It is this ability to play with possibilities and explore connections which yields the power of models and metaphors. Whether a particular model is a good one or not depends on how well the unknown system can inherit the laws and properties of the relevant supertypes.

The reason why the solar system can be used to model the atom is that the two systems have many supertypes in common. The most important supertype is that of a central force field system (see Figure 5.4). By placing the atom and the solar system under this common supertype, they inherit meta-properties of central force fields in general, e.g. the central force field law, conservation of angular momentum, energy levels, and so on. The fact that the model system and the system being modelled inherit the same meta-properties from their common supertypes explains how analogies are generated as a result of locating the unknown system in the type-hierarchy. A central force field system has a centre and satellites; so does the solar system and, now, the atom. Any relationship between parts in the supertype is inherited by the subtypes. Hence sun/nucleus = planets/electrons, gravitational energy/orbital energy = planets/electrons, mass charge/electric charge = planets/electrons, and so on.

But not planets/electrons = crater/what?, for having craters or a relationship between craters and something else cannot be inherited from the properties of central force fields. In other words the problem of filtering out negative analogies is no longer an obstacle in the analogy, because the 'negative' properties of the model system are not represented at the level of the supertype. Properties like craters, the possession of moons and an atmosphere are not part of the general higher-order supertypes for the solar system and thus are not inherited by the atom. Rather, the solar system is a type of structure based on a central force field. The basis of comparison between the solar system and anything for which it can serve as a model, is that they are complex physical systems which are instances of a central force field. The central force field law holds for each subtype, including gravitational and Coulomb fields. Thus, the fact that natural kinds inherit laws and other supertype properties is what generates the mapping in an analogy. Hence, there is no need to rule out the negative analogies *ad hoc*, because the common supertypes will generate only positive analogies between the systems.

Clearly the dependence is reversed from the comparison view of models. Instead of the model and the system modelled being compared for similarities thus basing the model chosen on analogies, the analogies are generated via inheritance and the laws contained in the supertypes from the hierarchy in which the systems are located. The analogical mapping of the sun/nucleus and planets/electrons appear at the bottom-most layer

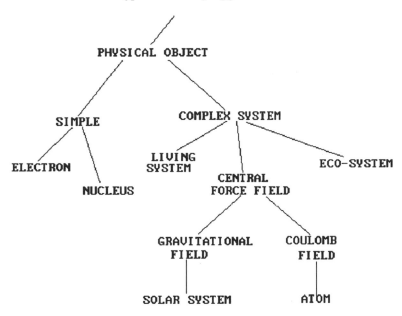

Figure 5.4. A partial type-hierarchy for the atom and the solar system

of the hierarchy. But these analogies only fall out as a result of the inheritance relation and the laws and properties of the supertypes. This is what we mean by similarity between models being just the tip of the iceberg.

We can also see now why the racing car analogy for explicating the atom is a trivial one. The law *describing* the motion of the racing car is mathematically the same as that of the solar system because the car is on an elliptical track. If we just compare systems for possible structural isomorphism, then the racing car and the solar system are equally good models for the atom. But we are not simply dealing with similarities between the local (bottom-most) properties of the two systems. Instead the solar system is a source for a planetary model for the atom because both are subtypes or instances of the same general supertype. They both inherit their properties from the central force field law. Once more it is the inheritance relation and the structure of the hierarchy which generates the analogy, not the isolated comparison of properties at the lowest level. Thus analogies are only as good or as plausible as the hierarchy (or theory) in which the model and modelled system are embedded.

According to our picture, the model system and the system being modelled are really instantiations of our lowest subtypes in a hierarchy, and the explaining theory incorporates them both. Thus, if we look at the structure of a scientific theory we find that models are already built in. To get rid of the models would mean getting rid of the theory as well. For example, with the Bohr model of the atom, why is the solar system a model for the atom? The reason is that there is an already existing ontology of the world where the concepts and relationships for the notion of a central force field are already instantiated. This ontology can be expressed in the structure and inheritance relations of a type-hierarchy. Both solar systems and atoms will be subtypes of central force field type and will inherit all the properties of such a field. In a way, the entire hierarchy is our theory of the world, and the meaning of a particular hypothesis within the theory will depend upon the positions held by its concepts. Thus, on this view, model systems are an inextricable part of a theory insofar as a scientific theory is instantiated by orderings of natural kinds. This means that models cannot be discarded as part of science without removing the theoretical framework in which the model systems are located as well.

There is another aspect of the indispensability of models which has apparently been overlooked by those who have debated their necessity. We have pointed out elsewhere that the use of models differs from other ways of forming hypotheses about a system by analogically displaying or simulating its behaviour (Harré, 1988: 120-1). On the other hand, instruments, the other main device for doing science, measure the behaviour of the system under a variety of circumstances by interacting with it. The important point here is that studying the behaviour of a system by studying a working model of it is 'counterfactual' in a way that the use of measuring instruments to discern the behaviour of a system is not. The reactions of an instrument are relevant only when the actual behaviour of the system in question is being measured. But imagining the behaviour of a model, or running an engine that has been constructed on the laboratory bench or in a computer, gives you 'counterfactual' information. It tells one how the system would behave under any of an indefinite variety of circumstances. For example, a thermometer is used to tell the temperature of an actual gas in certain definite circumstances. It cannot be used to find out what temperature it would be under other circumstances, particularly circumstances that are unable to be replicated in the laboratory.

Models, then, allow us to do experimentation that instruments cannot possibly afford, for with instruments we have to produce the actual behaviour in order to get experimental results. With models, on the other hand, we are allowed to make predictions independently of any interactions with the system under investigation. Let us take a system where it is theoretically impossible to come up with an instrument to measure some salient feature. Nevertheless, with models, we can directly 'observe' the behaviour of that system by observing the behaviour of the model, by making use of the similarity relations licensed by the relevant type-hierarchy, and then we can see whether that behaviour fits with what should be expected in the imagined circumstances, in accordance with other confirmed principles.

The belief, then, that we can predict and experiment without models is a myth, for there are certain types of experimentation that are possible only by means of models. Our ideas about what happened during the first few minutes of the history of the universe, just after the 'Big Bang', are a perfect case in point.

7. Conclusion

In summary, the rejection of the traditional comparison view of models and analogy and the advent of type-hierarchies representing the ordering of natural kinds in a scientific theory has the following results for scientific models. First of all, models are seen to be both indispensable to science and irreducible to formally ordered sets of propositions. The ontological and metaphysical models represented by the type-hierarchy cannot be reduced to propositions and deductions according to the logicist or deductive-nomological model. Rather, theories are seen to be based on chunks of type-hierarchies. Of course, anything can be *described* in propositions whose form can be represented in the predicate calculus once the structure and ordering of models and kinds is already developed. But such a description is only a rigid and static snapshot. The models themselves are not static sets of propositions. They are instead dynamic representations of objects – natural kinds and relations between them, and the type-hierarchy *generates* salience and similarity through inheritance and the empirically determined ordering of these kinds.

Furthermore, models give us another means of experimentation that can go beyond that which is possible by instruments alone. Models give us counterfactual information about the system under investigation; information about how the system would behave in a variety of circumstances, not just the current actual one. In scientific theories directed to describing states of affairs occurring among entities and structures in circumstances in which it may be impossible to use instruments to measure the behaviour of the system in question models allow us to proceed beyond the frontiers of the actual. In studying very rapid chemical reactions, for instance, models become truly indispensable.

We will learn in Chapter Six that Tarskian correspondence as an account of truth in science must be replaced by a limiting case of a similarity relationship between a model and the system modelled. In other words, we cannot have a semantics of verisimilitude and truth unless our theories include models. Thus we have a semantics more akin to the Giere-Hesse program. Models cannot be reduced to sets of Tarskian correspondences or literal truths. On the contrary, we maintain that truth is to be explicated in terms of the degree of similarity between model systems and the actual systems that they represent. One outcome of our position is that literal truth is a limiting case of approximate truth, that the literal can be thought of as a limiting case of the figurative when the links of a figurative type-hierarchy collapse into literal links.

Our conception of theories and models has also enabled us to solve the problem of how relevant positive and negative analogies are generated using the inheritance relation instead of *ad hoc* measures. The structure of the hierarchy and the ability of a natural kind to inherit the meta-properties and laws of higher-order kinds determines what mapping there will be in an analogy. Thus we no longer have the problem of filtering out the negative analogies since they are not even generated as part of the model. This is because inheritance replaces structural isomorphism in determining analogies. Likewise trivial and non-trivial analogies are distinguished in terms of the hierarchy.

Again inheritance replaces similarity comparisons, yielding only material analogies.

Furthermore we can see that analogies are only as good as the ontology (type-hierarchy) in which they are embedded. Our metaphysical models as represented by the type-hierarchy are determined empirically rather than logically or *a priori*. The kinds of models and explanations we come up with for a particular phenomena will be relativised to the kinds of entities, properties and interactions that make up the entire ontology of our world. Both model systems and real systems are embedded in the same type-hierarchy. Once the model is correct and it can be empirically confirmed, the analogy relation falls out naturally.

Thus we cannot evaluate analogies in isolation by simple comparisons without an underlying model. Simply comparing the properties between the lowest subtypes in the hierarchy is not rich enough to give us a non-arbitrary similarity mapping between the properties of sets of successive models, nor between each of these models and the world which it more or less resembles. Instead the analogies embodied in models involve the entire structure behind our lowest-level kinds. Models themselves are located at the lower end of the hierarchy, having an entire ontology submerged behind them.

We now can explain the notion of *salience* or why some aspects of a model are more important as similarities than others. According to our view, the important aspects of any model are determined by the ontological assumptions concerning natural kinds which are contained in the ordering and structure of the type-hierarchy. The higher-order types under which an instance of a natural kind falls constrain and highlight the features that are important for something to be a thing of that type. 'The natural-kind rules determine, in a general way, the features to be looked for in deciding whether a putative specimen should be recognised as an exemplar of the kind of being in question' (Harré, 1988: 130). The similarity relation is no longer serving as an unanalysed primitive but is unpacked and explained in terms of the relation between a natural kind and a higher-order kind. Furthermore similarity is seen to be a complex and non-symmetric relation which is derived from the content and structure of our ontological ordering of natural kinds.

We are on our way to unifying the various previously independent doctrines of scientific realism. The cognitive mechanism, which has previously been used to account for metaphor, provides us with the underlying theory of how one system can serve as a model for another. The information packed into type-hierarchies generates similarities and analogies in a non-arbitrary, structured way. We will learn in Chapter Six that the very same cognitive mechanism will provide us with a semantics of truth and verisimilitude. But this simply means that the language of models and metaphors is just as much a part of the language of science as the literal uses of words.

Scientific Realism and Truth

1. The traditional picture and its problems

According to convergent realism, scientific theories are meant as approximations to the truth, and in the limiting case scientific truth is correspondence with the facts (Popper, 1972). Correspondence has always been taken to be a relationship between a proposition and some state or condition of the world. The ultimate version of this standpoint is Wittgenstein's doctrine of 'picturing' laid out with such care in the *Tractatus*. Giere (1988: 106) insists that the verisimilitude of scientific theories cannot possibly be understood in terms of propositional truth, if by 'truth', we mean something like Tarski's attempt to characterise 'truth' as a meta-linguistic predicate of sentences. Correspondence is like pregnancy: it does not admit of degrees. How can a false proposition or theory be an approximation to the truth if it is admitted not to correspond to the facts? How can we say, for example, that quantum field theory, which is certain to be revised at some future time, is better at *not* corresponding to the facts than Newtonian mechanics? There is the same problem with the notion of 'fitting the facts'. How can something fit the facts better or worse if it is false, that is does not correspond to them? How can something do a better job of not corresponding? These questions seem unanswerable.

Yet just about every attempt to characterise verisimilitude uses correspondence as a basic unit of approximation. For example, the truth which is to be approximated in Tichy (1976), Oddie (1986) or Ninniluoto (1987) is the *whole* truth or nothing. For them each theory is to be assessed by how many true propositions there are in the total set of propositions that constitute the theory. Newton's physics includes a certain number of true propositions, but fewer than contemporary physics includes. This was the main idea of Popper's much criticised concept of verisimilitude. But the assessments of physical theories are not like that at all. In the first place the relationship between verisimilitude and truth is not that of part to whole. Propositions and theories that 'have verisimilitude' are not made of up bits of truth. They are not true at all. We agree with Giere's contention that the real reason why Newton's physics is closer to the truth than that of Galileo is that the model of the world Newtonian physics describes resembles the actual world better than that described by Galileo's physics. This is not a claim that could be cashed out by counting up the true propositions in each approach and comparing them with the total number of true propositions that would make up an accurate account of the actual world.

It is important to understand why propositional accounts of verisimilitude fail and why they should be replaced by weighted similarity comparisons between models and the world. According to Popper, the verisimilitude of a false theory depends on the number of true and false consequences that follow from it; in particular, the ratio of true consequences to false. Obviously, the greater the ratio, the greater the verisimilitude.

It is well-known among researchers on verisimilitude that such a theory falls short for two rather devastating reasons. It has been shown, for example, that for any false proposition, the number of true consequences *equals* the number of false consequences (Vetter, 1977); hence, any false theory has as much verisimilitude as any other! Not only that, Oddie (1986) has shown that Newton-Smith's version of measuring the ratio of true to false consequences meets a similar fate. According to Newton-Smith (1981), a false theory generates a series of true-false ratios, and of two theories, T and U, U has greater content relative to T when the limiting ratio of U is greater than that of T. Unfortunately, this characterisation of approximate truth will not do, as Oddie has shown, because one can always arbitrarily reconstruct the infinite series generated by U and T in such a way as to reverse their relative verisimilitude: under some enumerations, U is closer to the truth than T but T will come out closer to the truth under others. Oddie rightly concludes that 'the concept of relative content is not well defined'. (1986: 173) (Ironically, we will see below that Oddie's theory of verisimilitude has problems with infinities of its own.)

The most recent formal attempt to capture verisimilitude can be called the possible worlds approach. Its proponents include Ninniluoto (1987), Tichy (1976) and Oddie (1986). This approach partially characterises a theory in terms of the fundamental or basic states it ascribes to the world. Each combination of these 'atomic' states defines a possible world. A theory, then, picks out a set of possible worlds from the set of all possible worlds. If the world picked out happens to be the actual world, the theory is said to be true. On the other hand, if the theory does not pick out the actual world but other possible worlds, it is false. Although the theory may be false, it may not be completely false; it will contain some truth, depending how far the worlds picked out are from the actual world. According to the above, the distance between a possible world and the actual world is determined by their symmetric difference: the more basic states that differ between the possible world in question and the actual world, the more distant they are. To use Oddie's example, suppose there were only three basic states in the universe. Let them be hot, rainy and windy. Suppose it is, as a matter of fact, hot, rainy and windy. This means that there are eight possible worlds, one of which is the actual world:

	hot	rainy	windy	
W_1	T	T	T	actual world
W_2	T	T	F	
W_3	T	F	T	
W_4	T	F	F	
W_5	F	T	T	
W_6	F	T	F	
W_7	F	F	T	
W_8	F	F	F	

Let us suppose W_1 is the actual world. For Tichy and Oddie, the verisimilitude of a proposition is determined by the average distance between possible worlds in which it is true and the actual world. For example, in the above case, $h.-r$ would be a distance of .5 from the whole truth, $h.r.w$, because it is true in two possible worlds of distance 1/3 and 2/3 from the actual world.

Ninniluoto also uses symmetrical differences to determine the distance between the actual and possible worlds but he uses a mini-max function to measure the verisimilitude of a proposition, its verisimilitude being the average of the minimum and maximum distances of the set of possible worlds where the proposition holds (1987: 222-3). So, Ninniluoto agrees in spirit with Tichy and Oddie that verisimilitude is determined by similarity between possible worlds which are compared with respect to basic states. The major difference between them, it seems, is their selection of a distance function between worlds. There are other differences between them but, for our purposes, they will not be discussed here.

The possible worlds approach has been subjected to much criticism as of late. Strangely enough, much of it turns out to be from within the same camp. Likewise Miller (1978) has argued that the Tichy-Oddie approach can not possibly be linguistically invariant: that is, verisimilitude rankings are relativised to the language in which the theories are expressed. This would be a crowning blow if Miller turns out to be right about this, for verisimilitude, like truth, should be independent of conventional considerations.

However, we think an even more devastating criticism can be mounted. It is based on two intuitions: first of all, no false statement can be equally true or truer than the truth; and, secondly, the number of basic states in the universe should not, in itself, affect the verisimilitude of a proposition. The second can be put another way. Theories carve out chunks of the world which are semantically independent of one another. For example, the fact that there are one billion Chinese should not affect the truth or verisimilitude of the special theory of relativity unless the latter somehow entails something about the former. Likewise, the verisimilitude of Newtonian physics should not be affected by the existence or non-existence of temperature, entropy or other thermodynamic states, again, unless the existence of mechanical states entails the existence of thermodynamic states or *vice versa*. In other words, it will be shown that the possible-worlds approach, albeit a version of logical atomism, leads to a pernicious holism, one where the verisimilitude of a proposition becomes too dependent on the truth of other, completely irrelevant propositions (or states).

In order to see why this is so, let's return to the above weather example and calculate the verisimilitude of h as a function of the *number* of states there are in the universe, irrespective of what these states are. We will then compare the verisimilitude of h with other propositions, first using the Tichy-Oddie measure:

no. of possible states	h	$\sim h$	$\sim h.r$	$h \lor r$	$h \lor \sim r$	$h \lor \sim h$
$n=2$	.25	.75	.5	.5	.5	.5
$n=3$	.33	.67	.5	.39	.5	.5
$n=4$	.375	.625	.5	.41	.5	.5
$n=5$	.4	.6	.5	.433	.5	.5
.	.					
.	.					
.	.					
$\dfrac{n-1}{2n}$	$\dfrac{n+1}{2n}$					

Notice, straight away, that the verisimilitude of some contingent propositions is independent of the number of possible states while the truthlikeness of other contingent propositions is very sensitive to the number of possible states, *no matter what their content happens to be!* For example, h is about the weather while the 100th state might be about something entirely unrelated to the weather: say, the average height of the mountains on the moon. This does not mean that any state of affairs could not be related to any other when it comes to verisimilitude. It's just that their version entails that these states of affairs are related to one another, their relations being given *a priori*.

What is even more disturbing is that simply increasing the number of states, no matter what they may be, automatically leads to a decrease in the verisimilitude of a true proposition and a corresponding increase in the verisimilitude of a false proposition. If it is possible for there to be an infinite number of possible states in the universe, the results become even more ludicrous, for the verisimilitude h and $\sim h$ have the same limit when n goes to infinity, leading to a false proposition having as much verisimilitude as a true one!

This sensitivity to other, intuitively irrelevant truths leads to an even more disturbing result: we can readily find a case of a false proposition having more verisimilitude than a true one, simply by adding true conjuncts to a false proposition. Again, we simply increase the number of states in the universe:

	h	
~h.r	.5	.25
~h.r.w	.33	.33
~h.r.w.d	.25	.375
~h.r.w.d.x	.20	.40

A false proposition quickly accrues more verisimilitude, becomes truer than the truth, with just two additional true conjuncts, and things rapidly get worse for the true proposition after that.

Even though Ninniluoto uses a mini-max measure instead of averaging distances between possible worlds, his theory is open to the same criticisms, because the above calculations are exactly the same with his measure. The fault, then, does not lie with selecting the wrong distance measure for verisimilitude but with thinking of verisimilitude in terms of comparing possible worlds in the first place. This is so, we contend, for a very simple and obvious reason: when it comes to truthlikeness, we are simply comparing the thing or system the proposition refers to with the real thing or system; we are *not* comparing entire possible worlds in which these things or systems exist.

A more recent propositional approach to verisimilitude can be found in Kuipers (forthcoming). Instead of verisimilitude being a matter of counting up the truths of a theory and comparing it to the 'whole truth', approximate truth is now a function of explanatory success: two theories are equal in verisimilitude if and only if they equally explain established laws and data. Kuipers goes on to characterise a 'naive' version of this intuition in set theoretical terms.

The major reason why he calls the above version 'naive' is because of the difficulty of comparing entire theories with respect to verisimilitude if theories, laws and data are simply characterised as sets of propositions. While we can readily determine the approximate truth of a proposition by comparing it to the entire or whole truth, how are we to compare theories (sets of propositions) to the whole truth? How are we to compare theory structures?

Kuipers' answer is his refined version: two theories are equal if and only if they equally explain established laws and data; however, set-theoretical operations to determine their equality now take place over convex sets (sets that are closed for intermediates). In other words, sets of propositions which are now structured enable the desired comparison among theory structures.

It is impossible to do justice to Kuipers' theory in such a short space, partly because he brings so much technical ammunition to bear on verisimilitude. One problem we have with such an approach is that it is not clear how these technical moves give us any real insight into the nature of verisimilitude. One is reminded, here, of Wittgenstein's analogy between the technicality of ideal-language philosophy and a machine whose parts are going through many complicated motions, but we are left with no idea what function such a machine serves. We find it difficult to link the many technical moves Kuipers makes with respect to verisimilitude to the way it functions in science and in everyday life.

Even if his version is technically sound, we question the philosophical assumptions underlying the entire enterprise. In the first place, an anti-realist such as Van Fraasen or Laudan would be quick to point out that there exists an indefinite number of rival theories (models) that are equally successful at saving appearances. After all, theories in themselves do not explain laws and data; they require the addition of auxiliary hypotheses. But, they will maintain, it is always possible to construct another combination of a theory and auxiliary hypotheses in such a way that they explain the same set of propositions equally well. This is very much like the way Reichenbach (and Poincaré) maintained that a curved space where measuring rods maintain their length under transport can explain measuring results just as successfully as a flat space having the proper universal forces acting on these rods. Thus, theories that claim totally different things about the world – hence, they must have varying degrees of verisimilitude – are equally good at explaining one and the same set of propositions, whether that set is convex or not.

It is not even clear that a realist should welcome such a characterisation of approximate truth, especially if verisimilitude is to be the basic explanans of scientific progress. In other words, explanatory success is a symptom or an effect of getting closer to the truth, not a defining characteristic. The connection between verisimilitude and increased success in explanation is supposed to be an epistemic one, not a semantic one. So, we are afraid that by defining approximate truth in terms of explanatory success, Kuipers has confused semantics with epistemology. Simply put, if you characterise verisimilitude in terms of explanatory success, you can't use it to explain it.

Although it differs from those of Popper et al., Kuipers' theory is still in the propositional mode. Theories are sets of propositions and they explain sets of propositions. Verisimilitude among theories amounts to comparing sets of propositions. There's a moral to the above story: any propositional account of verisimilitude is doomed to failure, precisely because it is committed to characterising a theory as a set of propositions in the first place. The reason for this is very simple. Once theories are so characterised, we are locked into comparing sets of propositions, either by counting up direct or derived truths. True and false are the only relevant properties for comparisons. To repeat what we said above, verisimilitude intuitively amounts to comparing the properties of the thing (model) postulated by the theory with the actual item, how similar they are being a function of properties in common and their differences. So,the propositional approach is doomed to commit a version of the use-mention fallacy, precisely because it locks us into similarity comparisons between sets of propositions, and the only permitted features of such comparisons are truth and falsity. It is one thing to compare a gas in a laboratory with an ideal gas in terms of the relative interaction of the molecules, the radii of the molecules, etc. When a scientist is seeking a good gas model, why should he compile two lists of propositions, one depicting the gas model and the other the actual gas and then compare the two sets of propositions?

Replacing the strategy that is based on the idea that verisimilitude is a matter of comparing different sets of propositions with direct but weighted similarity comparisons between a model system and the real system it intends to capture gives us a wonderful clue on how to characterise truth. If verisimilitude and truth are related in such a way that one is an approximation of the other, then if we can come to understand what is meant by 'approximation' in this context, we can characterise truth as a limiting case of verisimilitude. We will maintain below that it is a limiting case of weighted similarity between objects. As it stands, although it seems unproblematic when described in common-sense terms, the traditional version of convergent realism is incoherent. The traditional correspondence conception of truth cannot be the limiting case of verisimilitude, since verisimilitude is defined, according to that point of view, in terms of truth. So, contrary to the programme of many philosophers of science, we claim that one should first try to understand what might be meant by verisimilitude and then characterise truth as the limiting case. We will show that scientific realism is indeed a metaphysical doctrine, but truth, realism and verisimilitude are all part of a single picture. They are not three separate doctrines that are merely patched together. It turns out that truth and verisimilitude are different aspects of a single metaphysics. This is a version of the realism and truth that those who have rejected the traditional correspondence theory as a basis for scientific realism could really live with.

But this means they were wrong to avoid truth and verisimilitude altogether. It can be shown that these concepts were always implicit in any version of realism. No one had been able to devise non-question-begging versions of the concepts of 'truth' and 'verisimilitude' that meshed with convergent realism. In this chapter we shall use the same notion of a type-hierarchy to provide a semantics of truth itself. This is based on the intuition concerning the relationship between verisimilitude and truth advanced above, that truth is a limiting case of verisimilitude or approximate truth. But unlike the way that many philosophers have attempted to arrive at a working relationship between truth and verisimilitude in which truth is a primitive concept and verisimilitude derived from it, we will show that both truth and verisimilitude can be based on the similarity relation, which is itself a function of the ordering of natural kinds – a metaphysical primitive.

The traditional correspondence theory explicates truth as a relation between a representation, picture or proposition and worldly states of affairs. In the theory we are proposing truth is not such a correspondence, but our judgment that a theory is true expresses an identity between types of states of affairs: the type of state of affairs demonstrated or picked out by the speaker's discourse or implicit in the model described in that discourse is the same type as that of the actual state of affairs. These are contingent type identities because which state of affairs is picked out in the type-hierarchy is independent of the type of any actual state of affairs. When the type picked out is similar to the actual type, we have verisimilitude. When we have a match, when there is just the one type, we have truth. Thus truth is a limiting case of verisimilitude.

2. Devitt and the rejection of bivalent realism

Devitt (1984), and we ourselves, have maintained that scientific realism is a metaphysical doctrine, that there is a mind-independent world to which we successfully refer by the use of our theories. We have reason to believe that successful reference is an essential feature of any working, progressive science. But can we rationally maintain these claims without having recourse to the traditional notions of truth and verisimilitude?

Although our criticisms of bivalence realism work for propositional versions of the correspondence theory of truth, we shall show below that there are other versions of the correspondence theory that are immune from them. In fact, the objective of this chapter is to show that there can be no version of realism without some version of truth and all that goes with it. Instead of redefining scientific realism in such a way as to avoid truth, the nicest strategy would be to redefine truth in a way that does justice to the notion and fits in with scientific realism. It will turn out that the strict all-or-nothing principle which seemed to be so characteristic of traditional views about truth and falsity was never a necessary feature of the generic concept of truth anyway: that is, the principle of bivalence is not universally valid but holds only in certain limiting cases. Once truth is assigned its proper role, that is once the proper semantics for the concept has been established, then the defence of a version of scientific realism that preserves the concept of truth can be achieved.

Devitt maintains that the realism issue 'Is science about a mind-independent material world?' should be settled before the semantic question namely 'What is the relation between theories and what they purport to describe?' and epistemic issues such as how we know whether one theory is a better account of that material reality than another, are tackled. This is because, he believes, realism can and should be completely explicated without bringing in truth or verisimilitude. This should not be taken to mean that he does not think that truth and verisimilitude are irrelevant to the scientific enterprise. Rather he thinks that they raise separate issues from the general question of the defence of scientific realism. Their development can take a separate course. For example, Devitt readily believes that a viable semantics of verisimilitude does not exist but this failure should not affect the viability of realism. The latter is not a doctrine defined in terms of verisimilitude but is a position held about the existence of an unobserved mind-independent world.

Not only is realism not concerned with semantical questions, but he also believes that the doctrine that maintains that truth and verisimilitude are necessary for characterising and explaining scientific progress is another myth. All we need to defend is the possibility of making successful acts of reference, without any semantic attachments.

Unlike ourselves, who remain sceptical whether any adequate account of propositional truth and a related account of verisimilitude of the right sort will ever be obtained, Devitt thinks that they are in the offing and that they are a legitimate part of the doctrine of realism. But for him they are logically independent doctrines.

It had been hoped that realism could be defended in a more modest form than heretofore, by basing it on reference. If scientific discourse and the associated experimental techniques enabled a human being to establish a physical link with a mind-independent world, whether the theory used to manage this was true or not, that would be enough. Truth and reference would, it was hoped, be established as completely separate achievements. In other words, the true business of realism or what realism is really about is metaphysics: our theories help us successfully to refer to a mind-independent reality, part of which may never be observed (Harré, 1986). This has nothing to do with semantics. We can successfully interact with that world despite the fact that all our theories are likely to be false. But is semantics really irrelevant to metaphysics? What if truth and verisimilitude are tied in with the metaphysical doctrines of realism? We shall try to show that the very way referential realists (including our younger selves) characterise realism smuggles in some version of the concepts of truth and verisimilitude.

The thesis that there is a way of defining a referential realism that is not dependent on the use of the concept of 'truth' itself depends on what has been called the 'principle of charity'. That principle allows one to say that two theories are coreferential even when some of the statements which they licence about the entities to which they refer are false. In particular it seems right to say that Thomson and Bohr were both referring to the same sort of thing when they referred to elementary electric charges, even though their 'pictures' of these entities were very different. It is clear that any version of referential realism is tied in with the principle of charity. But it is also clear that any application of the principle of charity requires judgments of verisimilitude. As B. Enc pointed out (1976), when we use theoretical terms to refer to real entities such acts must be subject to constraints. We cannot simply claim that the terms of a successful theory refer and that we can quite ignore the question of whether there are any descriptions derived from the theory that fit the referent. We do take that question seriously, and this is shown by the fact that the principle of charity is not applicable to just any case of successive theories. Why do we want to say that what Mendel was referring to by 'genetic factor' is 'roughly' the same thing as contemporary geneticists refer to by the expression 'DNA sequence on a chromosome', but we do not want to say that what people in the past meant by 'evil spirits' was the same as that which we refer to by the term 'viruses'? Nor would we want to admit that what chemists in the past meant by 'release of phlogiston' is the same process, 'roughly', as that which we refer to as 'oxidation'? The explanation of these strong intuitions can be found in the idea of fitting into a type-hierarchy. While Mendelian genes may not be strictly identifiable with a DNA sequence, they can be identified with something that highly resembles or comes close to being a particular DNA sequence in that each is a subtype of the same supertype, in the hierarchy of cellular constituents. Phlogiston cannot be taken to be similar to anything at the same level in a hierarchy of types of material stuff. As a substance of negative weight the phlogiston-type belongs in a different branch of the type-hierarchy of substances from oxygen and all those of positive gravity. Even if the type of entity that Mendel was referring to by the term 'genetic factor' is not of the same chemical type as any item in the complex biochemical world it can be identified with an idealised and much less biochemically complex type, where the type similarity is based on functional equivalence for instance. In scientific practice there is a notion of approximate identity of type that goes along with approximate truth of a theory. Putnam puts it this way:

> There is nothing in the world that exactly fits the Bohr-Rutherford description of the electron. But there are particles which approximately fit Bohr's description: they have the right charge, the right mass, and they are responsible for key effects which Bohr-Rutherford explained in terms of electrons ... The principle of benefit of the doubt dictates that we treat Bohr as referring to these particles. (Putnam, 1984: 145)

Referential realism requires that there be legitimate reference mediated by theoretical terms and that requires some form of the principle of charity. But the use of that principle requires an appeal to verisimilitude or approximate truth.

3. Similarity and type-hierarchies

We now turn to the development of a semantics for a concept of verisimilitude. As we have argued, verisimilitude is in essence a relation of similarity between one model and another and between models and some aspect of the world. If similarity is a complex, derivative relationship, in what way can one account for its features? In order to come up with an answer to this question and thereby develop a semantics of verisimilitude, we draw on those ideas from artificial intelligence and cognitive psychology that we have already informally introduced in the concept of a 'type-hierarchy'.

One reason why a semantics of theoretical verisimilitude has escaped analysis for so long is that philosophers have failed to come up with a correct representation of theories. Instead of theories being sets of propositions or even families of models, we claim they are in part depictions of natural kinds and the way they are ordered. We shall see below that both models and the real systems of which they are analogues are instantiations of natural kinds and are located at the lowest level of a hierarchical ordering of the relevant types in a model universe with which we represent our knowledge of the world. In fact it is the structures of type-hierarchies that provide us with the similarity differentiation which is missing in Giere's theory and in the naturalistic analyses we have ourselves offered in other places (Harré, 1986).

If the content of theories is adequately interpreted only by reference to systems of natural kinds, then type-hierarchies, which have been developed by researchers in AI, provide the perfect mathematical structure for representing that content, as we argued in Chapter Two. Secondly, if judgments of verisimilitude are based on resemblances between the models that theories describe and the real systems to which they refer, and if similarity depends on features or properties of things, we need a way to represent and measure this dependency. Thus it would be wise to take advantage of the empirical research on similarity metrics that can be found in cognitive psychology.

Thus the content of a theory is captured by a type-hierarchy. We briefly summarise here the type-hierarchy theory we introduced in detail in Chapter Two. According to the approach taken in AI, a type-hierarchy is a semantic net of concepts, representing types of varying specificity. The linkages between nodes represent relations between a type and its more specific subtypes. For example if mammal is a supertype in the hierarchy, whale, dog and elephant, etc, are among its subtypes, while sperm whale and humpback whale are, in turn, subtypes of whale. So, the various types of whale would be linked with whale, while whale, dog and elephant etc. are linked to mammal. A major feature of a type-hierarchy is the inheritance relation: those features which are characteristic of a supertype are also (inherited) features of each subtype. For example, a dog is a mammal and mammals nurse their young, so dogs nurse their young. Another relevant feature of a type-hierarchy is the transitivity of the subtype-supertype relationship: if humpback whale is a subtype of whale and whale, in turn, is a subtype of mammal, then humpback whale is a type of mammal. As a result, any subtype attribution generates a series of supertype or 'parental' attributions, depending on subtype-supertype linkages in the hierarchy. Thus (and taking for granted the implicit logical level of the ordinary language terms) if Snoopy is a beagle, then Snoopy is a dog, is a mammal, is an animal, is a physical object, and so on. Likewise, if the object swimming in the ocean is a mackerel, then it is a fish, is a sea animal, is an animal, and so on. The same can be said for all subtype attributions. This turns out to be the key to measuring the verisimilitude of a simple truth claim: it depends on what supertypes the predicate expression picks out in the type-hierarchy.

Why is this so? What does this have to do with verisimilitude? The answer is that the verisimilitude of a truth claim is a function of how similar the type of object selected by the proposition is to the type of the real thing. If we compare the verisimilitude of the statement that a certain animal (which is actually a blue-back whale) is a tiger shark with that of the statement that it is a dolphin, we can say that the latter identification is closer to the truth because a dolphin is of a type that is more similar to the type of a blue whale, the real thing, than the type of the other candidate.

The sense of 'similar' we have in mind, here, is type similarity. Two things are similar in that they are represented in the model world as subtypes of the same supertype(s): that is, in the real world they belong to the same natural kind. Unlike some other views of similarity, which treat it as an unanalysed and primitive relation, on this view, similarity between things is represented by the relative locations of the types under which they are being treated in a certain discourse on a hierarchy. Of course in different circumstances and with respect to different theories the way things fall under types will be different. Thus even if two things appear to be radically different, if they have a common supertype(s), they are similar in that respect(s). A whale may not look in the least like a dog but it is similar to a dog because they are represented in the model world as different types of mammals. But with respect to the science of hydrodynamics it is the ways in which the whale type is like the various fish types that define the salient concept of similarity, and hence of verisimilitude of theories of underwater propulsion, say. What is similar to what and in what degree is a meaningful question only relative to some type-hierarchy or other.

Let us illustrate this sense of similarity with the following abstract type-hierarchy:

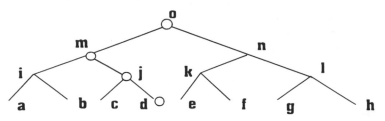

Figure 6.1. An abstract type-hierarchy

Since type similarity is a function of supertypes in common and those not in common, it is the overall structure of the hierarchy – its linkage – that determines to what extent two subtypes are similar or different. For example, if some object, x, is a d, then x is a j is an m is an o, according to the above hierarchy. It should be obvious, then, that the object most similar to x is a c, the next most similar is an a or a b, while the least similar would be either an e, f, g, or h. It is simply a matter of counting up the number of supertypes in common and subtracting those that are not in common. This number is a direct function of the links within the hierarchy, its overall topographical structure.

Individuals constitute the lowest level of the chosen hierarchy. Where an individual falls is an expression of 'episodic' as opposed to the semantic knowledge expressed in the hierarchies other levels. When we make a truth claim, we are placing an individual under a particular type. In this case, we are, in effect, placing x under d.

If type similarity were the only similarity comparison, it would follow that if x is, in fact, a d, then the claim 'x is a c' comes closest to the truth, while 'x is an a' and 'x is a b' are the next closest, and so on. A differently structured type-hierarchy would, naturally, lead to another ranking of truth claims. However, there are at least two more senses of 'similarity' to be taken account of. Two things may not display a type similarity but may have many non-essential attributes in common. A red pen is not a type of pen – *vis à vis* a fountain pen or a ball-point pen – and a red flower is not a type of flower, but the pen and the flower can resemble each other in that they are both red. The second sense of similarity, then, is attributive in case the attribute does not contribute to which type the object is, in relation to the chosen type-hierarchy. There is a third, quantitative sense of similarity. a is similar to b with respect to a given common attribute just in case the numerical measure, relative to a given choice of units, of the quantity in question that a possesses is close to the numerical value of the measure of that of b's. For example, while a whale resembles a dog in that they are both mammals, they are very dissimilar animals in terms of weight. On the other hand, a giant squid may be a sea animal which is more similar to a whale with respect to weight although it is an entirely different type of animal.

The functions used to measure attribute and quantitative similarities are discussed elsewhere. A good theory of verisimilitude must show how these senses of 'similarity' are combined, requiring the incorporation of attribute and quantitative similarities into type-hierarchies. A strong case can be made for the principle that type similarity is dominant when it comes to making judgments of verisimilitude. For example, if we had a mystery item in a box and it happened to be a red pen which weighed 2 ounces, of two guesses, say, a blue pen which weighs 2.5 ounces and a red banana weighing 2 ounces, we would say that the former guess came closer to the truth, even though it was mistaken on two counts.

However, because we are concerned with the connection between similarity and truth, we will focus on verisimilitude in terms of common supertypes. Not only do we contend that type similarity is a function of common supertypes, we also maintain that when it comes to comparing entire theoretical frameworks with respect to verisimilitude, some supertypes are more important than others. The importance of a supertype to verisimilitude is a function of the prominence of the role the supertype in question plays in capturing the *essence* of the actual item or subtype. In a biological case, perhaps being a mammal is more important for something being a dog than that it is fur-bearing. If so, we would weight their nodes in the representation world accordingly. Perhaps, a biological case can be made to show that some supertypes are more important than others when it comes to similarity of species. A biologist may be able to provide us with such a justification. It is important to realise that in the same way that the correspondence theory of truth involves linguistic conventions that fix the meanings of terms, deliberations concerning verisimilitude involve determining the importance or rankings of supertypes in the model. Rankings will vary according to the subject matter. We believe that determining these rankings is an empirical question. However, like the role of linguistic conventions in the correspondence theory of truth, once these rankings are fixed, the degree of verisimilitude assigned to a proposition is an objective matter.

At first glance it would seem that this account involves a kind of circularity. Don't we need a theory to determine the node weights in the type-hierarchy? But the weighted nodes of a type-hierarchy are supposed to be constitutive of the content of the theory. It is true that weighting the supertypes does depend on theory, but so long as the theory on which the weighting depends is logically independent of the theory represented by the type-hierarchy whose nodes are being weighted, questions are not begged. One type-hierarchy is being used to refine the structure of another. For example, if the 'weighting' theory that tells us it is biologically more important to be a mammal than to be fur-bearing when it comes to being a dog is independent of the way we classify animals – for example it may be a theory about reproductive advantages in the conditions of an ice age – then using the second theory to weight the nodes of the animal taxonomy does not lead to circularity.

We have seen that 'type similarity' does not denote a simple comparison of properties. On the contrary, it is a very complex concept, with an internal structure which goes beyond the logic of a simple dyadic predicate. In fact recent work on the similarity relationship even questions the age-old belief that it is a symmetrical relationship. The basic intuition on which our analysis of the similarity relation depends is that type similarity is a function of common and differing supertypes. The question then becomes 'What function?' This is where research in cognitive psychology comes in, for psychologists have investigated such functions, with interesting results. For example, Tversky (1977,1987) developed a formula for measuring similarity in terms of properties in common and properties which one object has but the other lacks:

$$S(a,b) = \Theta f(A \cap B) - \alpha f(A - B) - \beta f(B - A).$$

This formula says that similarity between a and b is a function of properties in common to a and b but it also depends on their symmetrical difference, i.e. those features a has but b lacks and *vice versa*. If Θ is much larger than α and β, then common features are more important than the symmetrical difference. This depends on the situation, what types of things are being compared, etc. It is clear, however, that if the above formula is correct, $S(a,b)$ is not symmetrical, except in the special case when $(\alpha - \beta)f(A - B) = (\alpha - \beta)f(B - A)$ (Tversky, 1977: 333). Just as important, the value of the constants in the above formula can be experimentally determined, which is nice, for it enables us to study the similarity relationship empirically. We have ourselves developed a similar measure of the strength of analogy, which also depends on a function of common and distinctive features (Harré, 1986).

4. An illustration of the type-hierarchy approach to verisimilitude

Suppose something is swimming in the ocean and many different identifications of the object have been made. It is identified as a blue whale, a dolphin, a mackerel, a humpback whale, a tiger shark, a seal, a giant squid, a bear, a dog, and so on. If, in fact, a blue whale is swimming out there, then the first identification is the target truth while the other false claims are more or less close to the truth. We will now use the above theory of verisimilitude to provide a semantic measure of their respective proximity to the truth. Each claim serves to identify a simple model of the object in question. Put in terms of models the question of verisimilitude becomes which model is more similar to the target object than another.

Though numbers are to be assigned to truth claims in accordance with the position of the type of each model in the type-hierarchy, they are only to have significance as a means of comparison. Their absolute value has no significance. Likewise only the qualitative or categorical notion of similarity and the resultant ranking of verisimilitude will be considered here, i.e. we are only counting similarity between different types of things *vis à vis* the attribute and quantitative similarity relations implicit in the type-hierarchy which is actually in use in making the judgments. For example, we are not to count the fact that an elephant resembles a blue whale with respect to size and weight.

We are going to assume, for the sake of simplicity, that properties the candidates for degrees of verisimilitude have which the target animal lacks will not count against the verisimilitude of the representation of the object in the model world. For example, that a dog has legs but a blue whale does not will not affect the verisimilitude of the claim that a dog is swimming in the ocean. So, on this account, the verisimilitude $\beta = 0$ in the Tversky formula. According to the above theory of verisimilitude, we need a type-hierarchy – a biologically-based hierarchy – in order to decide the truthlikeness of the above eight rival truth claims.

There is no way of answering the question of what the real ordering of biological types is. This will depend on the purpose to which this or that type-hierarchy is to be put. For illustrative purposes any arrangement of types will do. The rival truth claims can be ordered in a way which correspond to subtypes in the following type-hierarchy (Figure 6.2):

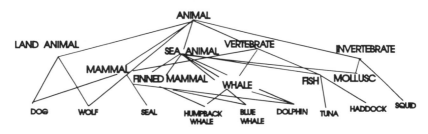

Figure 6.2. An oceanic type-hierarchy

Applying the modified Tversky formula to this hierarchy, we can calculate the degree of verisimilitude of a truth claim simply by adding up types in common between the model and the target animal for similarity and subtracting the supertypes that blue whales pick up but the candidate in question does not as represented in the model world. The result is this ordering of verisimilitude between the above rival truth claims (Figure 6.3):

Blue whale = 7 = 'truth'
Humpback whale = 6 Dolphin = 6
Seal = 5
Shark = 2   Mackerel = 2   Bear = 2 Dog = 2
Giant squid = 0

Figure 6.3. Tversky measures of verisimilitude of possible models

It is true that there is not much differentiation among the values of verisimilitude in this example. But this can be attributed to the lack of naturalistic complexity in the above type-hierarchy. A more complex one, especially one where the nodes are weighted, would lead to different scores for, say, shark and bear, bear and dog, and so on. If we are to test the above theory of verisimilitude by comparing the resultant rankings with our intuitions in detail, we would require a very sophisticated type-hierarchy together with such other hierarchies as are necessary to weight the nodes in the hierarchy which is the prime source of our models. In addition to this, it is not at all clear what the proper scale factors in the above Tversky formula should be for such a comparison in a biological context. Again, this would require an empirical study.

In the above animal type-hierarchy the models and the real system are located at the lowest level. This is what we meant by our remark in Chapter Five that the family of models being just the tip of the iceberg when it comes to theory. Families of models are not formed by making direct comparisons with respect to similarity. On the contrary, the process is the reverse. The relationship among natural kinds, which is represented by a type-hierarchy, generates type similarities. In this way we learn how models are grouped and which systems are better suited as models for a target particular system.

5. Truth and verisimilitude

What is the relationship between truth and verisimilitude?

In light of the above characterisation of verisimilitude, the most natural answer is that we have truth when the representation of the object or state of affairs in the model world referred to is exactly similar to or the same as the one picked out in the type-hierarchy by the speaker. In other words, truth is a limiting case of verisimilitude. It is a representation of a real relation between real things by a relation between model things. Statements inherit the degree of truth of the structure of the relevant fragment or chunk of the relevant type-hierarchy. If we let '*a*' and '*b*' respectively denote the type of state of affairs picked out by the speaker and the type of the actual state of affairs, and '*S*' stand for type similarity:

'*a*' is the true identification if and only if $Sa,b = Sb,b$.

If now we denote the object in question as '*A*' the statement '*A* is an *a*' is true because it inherits the truth of the fragment of the type-hierarchy. It can be seen how the above equality is a limiting case of the Tversky formula.

Although propositional truth has been defined, here, indirectly in terms of verisimilitude, the characterisation is in keeping with many versions of the naive correspondence theory, albeit these versions differ significantly from the correspondence theory which has been so heavily criticised. To illustrate this point let us take a closer look at Austin's (1970: 122) version of the correspondence theory of truth. He writes:

> A statement is said to be true when the historic states of affairs to which it is correlated by the demonstrative conventions (the one to which it 'refers') is of a type with that which the sentence used in making it is correlated by the descriptive conventions. [Later on in the same paper, he warns us that truth, like freedom, is an ideal, that] there are various *degrees* and *dimensions* of success in making statements: the statements fit the facts always more or less loosely, in different ways on different occasions for different intents and purposes (ibid.: 130).

Here, it is clear that Austin treats truth as a limiting case of verisimilitude in more or less exactly our sense.

In 'How to talk: some simple ways' we learn that correspondence is much more complex than a simple map between a sentence and the world. Correspondence or fitting the facts is actually a four-way relationship: (1) an 'is a' link between the subject and predicate of a sentence; (2) a referential link between the subject expression and the state of affairs named; (3) a referential link between the predicate expression and the type of state of affairs picked out by it; and (4) a matching relationship between the type of object picked out by the speaker and the type of the state of affairs. This is illustrated by the analysis of the claim '1227 is a rhombus' (ibid: 138).

'1227'	'is a'	'rhombus'
(I-word)	(assertive link)	(T-word)
reference		sense
item/type	natural link	sense
(sample)	(match)	(pattern)

Figure 6.4. The structure of a truth claim

We see that (4) is a type similarity comparison between the actual type of affairs and the type selected by the speaker. The key relationship when it comes to a sentence fitting the facts, then, really occurs at the lowest level *vis à vis* the vertical links. Contrary to the usual emphasis placed on the relationship between sentences and the world, it is type identity or type resemblance – a metaphysical relationship – that generates correspondence (cf. ibid: 146-7; 160-2).

In a recent publication Vision (1988) makes this point even clearer. At the heart of his defence of the correspondence theory of truth is a distinction between the truth conditions of a statement and its truth value: a statement picks out a particular situation or state of affairs *independently* of its truth value, i.e. what type picked out or discriminated by the speaker has nothing to do with its actual truth or falsity (ibid.: 129ff). For example, one may claim that there's a dolphin swimming in the ocean near our boat, but before we can evaluate the speaker's claim we must first pick out the right type of animal, the statement's identity, in our conceptual space. On the other hand, the truth value of the statement is a function of the relationship between the type of situation picked out by the speaker and the actual type of affairs.

This means that 'the truth of a statement is a matter of a particular situation belonging to a certain type. (To avoid possible misunderstanding we might add "or being identical with that type")' (ibid.: 126). So, according to Vision's vision of truth:

A statement made with sentence S is made true *by the specific state of affairs which S as used demonstrates being of a type discriminated by the type of S*, qua sentence (ibid.: 128).

If he is right about this, it is type identity: that is, token a = token b if and only if they are tokens of a single type, that underlies the correspondence theory of truth. Once more, correspondence between a sentence and the world is explicated in terms of type identity in the world. We have claimed that the above versions of the correspondence theory can be translated in terms of verisimilitude and type-hierarchies. All we need do is to introduce a state of affairs or situation type-hierarchy. Such a hierarchy serves as a 'truth filter': that is, it enables us to determine if two statements are asserting the same truth.

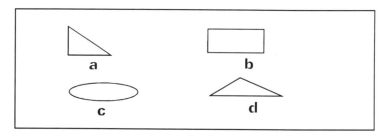

Figure 6.5. A simple geometrical type-hierarchy

For example, in Figure 6.5, while a and d may differ in size and shape, 'a is a triangle' and 'd is a triangle' assert the same truth in that they predicate the same type of figure: that is, both sentences pick out the same node in a geometrical figure type-hierarchy. Any other information about a and d is simply irrelevant to the truth of the above statements. It is filtered out by the situation type-hierarchy.

There are many important conclusions we can draw from characterising truth in terms of a state of affairs type-hierarchy. In the first place, the very same metaphysical mechanism of an ordered system of natural kinds underlies both truth and verisimilitude. Truth and verisimilitude are related in terms of this hierarchy: while verisimilitude involves the relative location of types of states of affairs, truth is simply their type identity. But such an account of truth and verisimilitude has a metaphysical underpinning. Our primitives are natural kinds, and it is nature which in the end determines the way they are ordered and their identity relations. Finally, we have a turnabout on the dependence of truth and realism. Instead of defining realism in terms of truth (as correspondence), truth is now characterised in terms of realism (the ordering of natural kinds).

In Chapter Five we distinguished figurative and literal language in terms of the results of masking operations on a dynamic type-hierarchy. We noted that one major difference between literal and figurative type-hierarchies is that the latter possesses more linkages among type nodes, more interconnectiveness among semantic domains, than the former. It is this feature of a metaphor type-hierarchy that allows for the transference of properties via inheritance from one semantic domain to another or from the model system to the system being modelled. Now, the transition from verisimilitude to truth is really mirrored by a 'collapse of the type-hierarchy'. In the case of verisimilitude, we are comparing different subtype systems – the subtype picked out by the truth claimer and the actual type – in terms of similarity by applying the Tversky formula to weighted supertypes. Here, in the case of approximate truth, the subtype picked out by the speaker and the actual subtype differ, along with their supertype 'parents'. In the case of truth, however, we have literal truth instead of metaphorical or approximate truth. In terms of the Tversky formula, $Sa, b=Sb, b$, i.e. the subtype picked out by the truth claimer is the same as the target truth, and so are their supertypes. Thus for literal truth, the hierarchy collapses to a bare minimum of nodes and links.

6. Conclusion: truth and scientific realism

We have argued elsewhere that natural kinds and their orderings are an essential feature of any variety of realism (Harré, 1986: 121-3). The metaphysical structure underlying a theory which determines its content is not a network of concepts but a hierarchy of natural kinds: 'Conceptual systems as embodied in the cognitive objects that underlie particular moments of explicit theoretical discourse are indeed structures of interconnected parts, but their organisation is hierarchical' (ibid.: 220-1). If so, this representation of theories already provides us with a mechanism for truth and verisimilitude.

We have seen that Devitt and others have focused on realism as a metaphysical doctrine. Devitt puts it this way: 'I have identified under the term "Realism" a doctrine that is a little epistemic but is largely metaphysical. I shall argue that this doctrine is quite distinct from any substantive semantic doctrine' (Devitt, 1984: 35). Yet, how does he characterise realism, scientific or otherwise?

> Realism: Tokens of most current common-sense, and scientific, physical types objectively exist independently of the mental.

If we have been right about verisimilitude and truth, the central thesis of Devitt's book, viz. that realism has nothing to do with truth, is lost. Admitting that there is a pre-categorised world of physical types *ipso facto* provides the mechanism for generating truth and verisimilitude. We have seen that type-hierarchies are what 'truth' and 'verisimilitude' are all about.

In order to emphasise how 'semantic-laden' these type-hierarchies are, we maintain it is conceivable, under certain circumstances, to be a *convergent* realist after all, without having to insist on the mind-independent world thesis. We have argued elsewhere for the importance of taking physical reality as an *Umwelt*, that ever-changing region of the 'whole world' which is available to us just in so far as we have the instruments and the conceptual resources to make it available to us. In other words, it is not clear to us that the notion of a 'mind-independent world', with all its problems, is a necessary feature of realism. There is a distinction to be made between *truth* realism and *object* realism. Quantum mechanics and the new unified theories are just such a case in point. Many physicists have come to believe that these new theories – e.g. grand unified theories, string theory, etc. – are getting closer and closer to the truth. In fact many believe, rightly or wrongly, that these theories will eventually reach the rock bottom of nature, revealing natural kinds which have no constituents at all. Not only that, these theories are highly metaphysical, for it may be some time before they are confirmed by observation, if at all. Even so, many theoreticians feel that to develop such theories is 'the only game in town'. Here, at the cutting edge of physics, we have a version of convergent realism with all the semantic and metaphysical trappings we have been delineating. Yet it is well-known in a community of physicists and philosophers increasingly influenced by the subtleties of Bohr's approach to the interpretation of physics that the metaphysics of these theories may be incompatible with the thesis that they describe a mind-independent world. Showing their compatibility or incompatibility with the old picture of an 'objective' physics is one of the most important problems in the philosophy of physics today (Brown and Harré, 1990). But the incompatibility of the metaphysical foundations of these theories with the assumption that their content is a mind-independent world should not detract from the fact that it is possible that they are getting at deeper depictions of nature. In a more subtle way they are getting closer to the truth. In other words, one can maintain that there is a truth 'out there', waiting to be discovered, but such a truth is defined in terms of type-hierarchies of things and structures that are brought into being as affordances of an instrument-dependent micro-world.

Giere could accept such a possibility because those models that best resemble the actual world may have instrument-dependence packed in. Even so, for him, it is the relationship between the model and the actual system that really matters when it comes to approximation. Because of this, he argues, realism can and should be characterised without propositional truth. 'The relationship that does the heavy representational work is not one of truth between a linguistic entity and a real object, but of similarity between two objects, one abstract and one real. From this point of view the difficulties with the standard view arise because it tries to forge a direct semantic link between the statements characterising the model and the world – thus eliminating the role of models altogether' (Giere, 1988: 82).

Giere is absolutely right that the 'heavy representational work' is done by similarity between a model and the real system. But this version of the correspondence theory is not new. It has been proposed by Austin, Vision, et al., although they do not express it in quite those terms. We have seen above how they characterise 'correspondence' or 'fitting the facts' in a very complex way. They certainly do not treat these notions as referring to a simple mapping between linguistic entities and the world. On the contrary, we have learned above that 'correspondence' is not a primitive mapping relation but a function of matching between types. It is this matching that generates the 'correspondence' between the proposition and a state of affairs. But then there is little or no difference between these non-Tarskian versions of the correspondence theory of truth and what Giere advocates in the above quote. He and many others have simply failed to realise that other versions of the correspondence theory of truth can be invented.

We can apply these insights directly to another difficult problem that has confronted those seeking a semantics of verisimilitude. How should we set about ranking laws in terms of proximity to the truth. On what basis do we take it that, as anyone who understands the history of the physics of gases would agree, van der Waal's law is closer to the truth than the ideal gas law? A detailed answer to this and similar questions is beyond the scope of this book, but we can sketch out an answer in the light of our program. We contend that so long as one continues to think of laws as propositions, and tries to assess their relative verisimilitude by how well each putative law corresponds to the facts, the task is hopeless. We have argued that laws are not best thought of as propositions, though they are capable of propositional expression. Laws are invariant relations between properties. We have argued that judgments of verisimilitude are based on similarity comparisons between the type of object referred to by a scientist and the actual type of the corresponding object nature. The relative verisimilitude of laws can be thought of in the same way, namely as the degree to which the relationships between properties depicted in relevant theories resemble the actual relationships between properties in nature. Since most lawlike relationships are expressed by mathematical functions, we need a weighted type-hierarchy of functions. Such a hierarchy might look something like this:

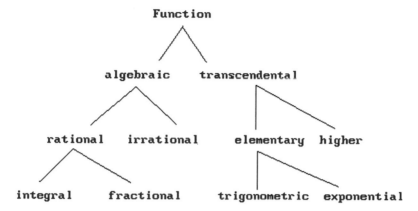

Figure 6.6. A type-hierarchy of functional relationships

The reason why the force law of the Special Theory of Relativity is closer to the truth than the Newtonian force law is that while the latter is a simple linear relationship between force and acceleration, with mass as a constant, the former involves a more complicated relationship between force, mass and acceleration. If it is closer to the truth it will pick up more supertypes in common with the actual relationship than the Newtonian law.

To complete an assessment of this kind fully would involve much more than we have included in the above sketch. For example, how much consideration should be given to other variables that have been excluded from the expression of a law; ought we even to allow such context-independent comparisons which have been made without taking into account the relative verisimilitude of the theories in which these laws are embedded? However, we contend that any more adequate procedure will simply involve the consideration of more complex type-hierarchies, rather than any difference in principle.

Our final application of the type-hierarchy point view is to the question of whether a contradictory theory can be nearer to the truth than another, consistent rival. There are many instances of this phenomenon in the history of physics, the most startling perhaps that of the superiority of Newton's physics over Galileo's despite the internal contradictions of the former, contradictions that did not become obvious until the mid-eighteenth century in

Maclaurins' paradox and the criticisms in Boscovich's *Theoria*. It is widely held today that relativity theory is inconsistent with quantum mechanics; yet the logical conjunction of the two creates a theory which is acknowledged to be nearer the truth than any possible rival.

If theories are expressed in terms of type-hierarchies, we can also explain how an inconsistent theory can be closer to the truth than a consistent but false theory. The inconsistency can be traced to links in the hierarchy that either yield subtypes that have inconsistent 'parents' or 'parents' whose meta-properties are incompatible. For example suppose the true theory relative to a given subject matter can be represented by a type-hierarchy laid out as the bold lines in Figure 6.7. The inconsistent theory is the true theory plus one additional link between subtype R and supertype Q, the fine line.

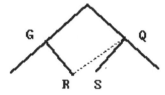

Figure 6.7. A type-hierarchy for an inconsistent theory

Let us add that R inherits T from G and U from Q, and that T and U are incompatible properties. 'R is T' and 'R is not T' would both be true. Nevertheless the inconsistent theory differs from the true theory by one link only, making it closer to the truth than any other false theory. An 'Escher' fork, though it is an 'impossible object' is more like a real fork than is a spoon!

The point is that once we have devised a semantics for truth and verisimilitude in terms of a common mechanism of orderings of natural kinds, a mechanism represented by type-hierarchies, then an account of a model approximating or matching reality is also an account of verisimilitude and truth. One cannot have one without the other.

We now have a theory of truth that is essential to any version of realism. If one is to be a realist, of no matter what variety, one must have a natural way to accommodate truth and verisimilitude. We believe that in this chapter we have provided just that.

CHAPTER SEVEN

Conditionals and the Modalities of Scientific Discourse

1. The problem of contrary-to-fact conditionals

Throughout this book we have argued that though it is possible to express some of the content of scientific knowledge and belief propositionally and often convenient to do so, there is an alternative method of knowledge representation which displays the structure and nature of that knowledge in a more perspicuous way. Furthermore our proposals for an alternative formalism are closely tied to an ontology of types and natural kinds. In this chapter we turn to an important feature of the propositional expression of scientific knowledge, namely its modalities. Our aim is to show how this feature of scientific discourse too can only be properly understood in our terms. The question to which this chapter is addressed could be put like this: what sort of ontology is required to explicate the modality of statements, such as the natural necessity we ascribe to laws of nature, within the general framework of a broad assumption of scientific realism?

Contrary-to-fact conditionals or counterfactuals, such as 'If I were to release this chalk it would fall', are some of the most important types of statements by which we express our everyday knowledge of how things generally are. They figure in all sorts of speech acts. They appear as commonsense explanations: for instance, 'If it were not for the fact that Mary overslept the day of the final she would have received an "A" for her philosophy course'. They can appear as warnings: for example, 'Don't drink the wine!' says Hercule Poirot; 'it *could* very well kill you, *mon ami*.' What all these statements have in common is that they seem to refer to possible states of affairs, and to express various 'strengths' of relations between them. In the case of Mary the implication is that attending the exam and getting an 'A' are necessarily connected, while Poirot's warning expresses only a probability. Philosophers of science have been aware of the fact that laws of nature seem to 'secrete' counterfactuals and that this fact is tied up with their modality. We shall approach the problem of specifying an ontology for the modalities of scientific knowledge through an examination of some of the proposals for making sense of these modalities which are already on the table.

There are two main ways in which philosophers have tried to explicate the meaning of counterfactual conditionals. One way is based on an analysis of the logical structures that seem to be exemplified in the propositional expression of conditional knowledge. We shall refer to this as the 'consequence' approach. Its ontological foundations are implicit. The other, which is based on an explicit ontology of real possibilities, we shall refer to as the 'possible worlds' approach. These two approaches exhaust the current ways in which the matter of modality is treated.

2. The 'possible worlds' approach to the interpretation of the modalities of scientific discourse

According to the possible worlds approach, 'If *P* were the case *Q* would have been true' (where '*P*' and '*Q*' express propositions) means that '$P \supset Q$' is true in the actual world and true in every 'nearest' world 'accessible' to the actual world. By 'accessibility' possible worlds theorists mean some degree of similarity to the actual world. Although many proponents of the possible worlds approach try to avoid its otherworldliness, Lewis (1973) has insisted that any belief in the truth of counterfactuals commits us to accepting the existence of possible worlds in addition to the actual one. To put the matter ontologically it would follow that a form of knowledge which required the use of counterfactual conditionals for its full expression would be committed to an ontology of possible worlds. So, if the full sense of a law of nature, in particular its natural necessity, could only be expressed, then physical science is and must be rooted in an ontology that admits the existence of possible worlds.

It is extremely unlikely that ordinary language users have possible worlds in mind when uttering sentences such as 'If that ball had been hit in Wrigley Field it would not have been a home run'. However, it does not follow that because someone does not think of something it is not presupposed in what they do say. A great deal depends on whether one is willing to accept the claims of modal logic to be the exclusive candidate for displaying the formal skeleton of all empirical discourses. While a case can be made that possible worlds semantics can account for modalities as they are expressed by means of the formal apparatus developed by Lewis et al., it is highly contentious that it provides a semantics of modalities for natural language. For example, if someone stated a possibility, that person would have to believe, in the sense that they would be required to assent to, the proposition that there is a possible world in which such a possibility *actually* exists. According to the possible worlds approach to say ' "X is possible" is true' makes sense only if one would also be prepared to say that there exists a possible world in which 'X is true'.

Modal systems have the power and virtues of other formal systems. What is at issue here is the ontology which it is claimed is the only way in which their meanings could be made clear. Or to put the matter in the terminology of Chapter Five, the claim we are disputing is the assertion that the only model for interpreting such systems is one in which the image of possible worlds is taken literally. There are several criticisms in the philosophical literature of the application of possible worlds semantics to the discourses of everyday situations. One class of counter-examples is due to Bennett (1974) and Sloate (1978). They have come up with convincing cases of intuitively true counterfactuals that would be true in more distant possible worlds than their counter-intuitive contraries, while the latter would be true in worlds more similar to the actual world than the worlds in which the seemingly acceptable counterfactuals would be true. This is surely a disturbing observation. We would certainly suppose that one would be more ready to accept a counterfactual statement as true in a world similar to our own than one as true in a more dissimilar world.

In response to the above criticism, Lewis (1991) attempts to save his theory, much as Bennett (1974) and Jackson (1977) suggest he would have to, by having recourse to laws. A counterfactual conditional is true if the corresponding conditional is true in the actual world and in every world closest or most similar to the actual world; however, causal relations determine what counts as sufficient similarity. In other words, no matter how much a possible world may appear to differ from the actual world, such a difference can be overlooked if it is independent of causal variables. For example, imagine a red weight suspended in a powerful gravitational field. We want to claim that were it released it would fall. A possible world in which a white weight is released in a weak gravitational field is not dissimilar, we would argue, in any relevant way, to the actual world, so it is true that the white weight too would fall if released. Why? The fact that in one world, the actual world, the weight is red and in the other, a colour-wise distant possible world, white, does not count against the counterfactual because colours simply play no part in the physics of gravitation. They are not variables in the relevant causal laws. It is the transworld generality of causal laws that determines whether or not a counterfactual is true.

Many feel that the above marriage of the possible worlds approach to the causal consequence view amounts to giving up the possible worlds theory of counterfactuals. The baroque metaphysics of possible worlds existing along with the actual world is redundant. It seems that we can simply use the relevant causal laws to provide us with a semantics of counterfactuals, without having to bring in possible worlds or even to compare them with respect to similarity. In fact we have incompatible notions of accessibility at work when the possible worlds theory incorporates causal laws. The causal law view could be used to define a kind of temporal accessibility. A future state is possible if there is a causal law which would link that state with some present state of the world. In these circumstances we could say that such a future is law-wise permissible. This is a far cry from defining accessibility in terms of degree of similarity to the actual world.

Before we turn to discuss the consequence approach, there is one more point worth making about the possible worlds approach in relationship to natural language. According to the possible worlds theory, there is a great difference in meaning between 'If P is true then Q is true' and 'If P were to be true then Q would be true'. According to that theory, the latter can only be made sense of within a metaphysics of existent possible worlds, whereas the former requires only the actual world. Yet it is not all that clear that there is such a semantical chasm in natural language. It is not at all clear that there is a real, ontic difference, as Lewis insists there is, between the situation referred to in 'If I were to release this chalk it would fall' and that referred to in 'If I release this chalk then it will fall'. We have asked many people, both philosophers and non-philosophers, what they think is different about the worlds presupposed in each case. Our informal survey shows that most people see these statements as implying only pragmatic differences: that is, differences in the likelihood of the consequential event coming about in this world. Sometimes this is expressed in terms of the strength of the intention of the speaker as to whether, in fact, he/she will, or wants to, release it. People simply do not recognise any deep differences in the physics of the situation. The analysis of counterfactuals presented below will reflect this lack of real difference between the ontological presuppositions of the two types of statements.

3. The 'consequence' approach and the problem of cotenability

The consequence approach – that is the idea that counterfactuals are true because the antecedent/consequent link in the counterfactual falls under the same causal laws as the antecedent/consequent link in the corresponding indicative conditional – is not free from difficulties. The most instructive for our purposes is the cotenability problem. According to the consequence theory, counterfactual conditionals are material conditionals that follow logically from laws, which are also conditionals, together with the relevant initial conditions. For example, 'If I were to strike this match, it would light' is analysed in the following way:

Suppose there are three 'standing' conditions necessary for a struck match to light. They could be the presence of oxygen (O), the match is dry (D) and the match is combustible (C). Let us represent the striking of the match by 'S' and its lighting by 'L'. Then the counterfactual conditional would be spelled out as follows:

(1) The following are true 'O & D & C & not-S & not-L' since in

the counterfactual case though the conditions did obtain no one struck the match and it didn't light.

(2) There is a law of nature that says 'If O & D & C obtain and S occurs then L'.

(3) It follows in propositional logic that 1 and 2 entail 'If S then L'.

Recall how Goodman (1965) has shown that such an analysis not only leads to conditionals which are reasonable, such as 3, but the very same premises yield other counter-intuitive conditionals. For example 1 and 2 also entail such a material conditional as 'If the match is struck (S), it will not be dry (not-D)'. But since, according to 1, to be dry is a necessary condition for the match to light, it now seems that we must accept that it will not light if struck. That is, it seems we must accept that S materially implies not-L. Goodman points out that in order to rule out the implication 'S materially implies not-D' we must establish the truth of another counterfactual: If the match were struck, it would remain dry. But in trying to establish this counterfactual we would run into the same problems. In other words, expressing the standing conditions for counterfactuals to hold by the use of material conditionals leads to a vicious regress.

The most natural defence for the consequent theorist to adopt is to deny anyone the right to use contrary-to-fact conditions (for instance, not-S and not-L) as premises in *any* derivation of a conditional. But, the critic will reply, in the counterfactual situation, which is, after all, what we are trying to deal with, these statements are *true*. We agree with this response.

To find an acceptable solution, it is important to represent the cotenability problem in a formal representation other than the propositional calculus. We believe that Goodman's problem can be rather easily solved if we change the formal framework. It will become clear that the real culprit is the use of the Frege-Russell logic for the expression of law statements, not the consequence approach. Let us look at the problem in another way. All we are given in the example are certain initial conditions for the occurrence of a phenomenon and laws relating these conditions to some expected outcome. It is also given that the event described in the consequent of the counterfactual does not or did not or will not occur. The worry is that the very occurrence of the antecedent may physically eliminate one of the enabling conditions for the event described in the consequent to occur. But if the consequent event would not come about in those very conditions, the corresponding counterfactual is false. It amounted to a claim that if the antecedent event did occur, the consequent event would. In the above case it remains *logically* possible (in the light of what is given) that the very act of striking the match a certain way will cause moisture to appear, preventing it from lighting.

'Backtracking' is another way to bring out the cotenability problem. Suppose we live in a deterministic universe. Given the laws of nature, with the exception of cases of the overdetermination of events, in which many different causal chains will serve to bring the event about, different pasts will lead to different futures. Striking the match in the future requires a past other than one where the match is not struck. But counterfactual deliberations are based on a past which does not lead to the match's being struck. How do we know that a past leading up to the match's being struck does not somehow prevent its being lit, for example, a past that places the match in position to strike the match box also causes pouring rain at the very same time and place at which the match is struck?

Solving the cotenability problem, expressed in this way, amounts to differentiating the kinds of laws and conditions that do lead to the elimination of one or more of the enabling conditions from those which do not. The only solution that could serve to resolve the problem in its Goodmanian version would have to be a syntactical one, since the problem is posed that way. But when the cotenability problem is expressed in terms of alternative paths to the future, a resolution depends upon considering the content of the relevant causal laws in relation to the processes that link the past, present and future.

4. An ontological approach to the interpretation of the content of laws of nature

We are seeking an account of modalities and counterfactuals that is free of any commitment to possible worlds but one that naturally follows from the approach to realism developed in the earlier chapters.

Instead of having an array of possible worlds, related by various degrees of similarity, as the knowledge base underlying modal sentences that are used in the discourses of everyday life, we hold that possible world semantics must be replaced by 'folk science': that is, by a knowledge base that consists of models of the structures and processes that represent what people believe occurs in the world. These can be verbally expressed in part as laws about the causal processes known or assumed to occur. Representations of the world and its processes are passed down from generation to generation. They are rarely formally expressed in textbooks. Of course, as research into the genesis of social representations has shown, many results of formal science can be and are incorporated into folk science. From our point of view the problem of modalities is how to come up with a way to represent folk theories and laws. Ordinary people do not speak predicate calculus; nor for that matter do natural scientists. Nor do ordinary people have possible worlds in mind when they are engaged modal discourse. We maintain, however, that they do have models of natural structures and processes in mind, and sometimes even the propositional expression of these models in laws or proto-laws. We shall show in section 5 how to incorporate them into the forthcoming analysis.

If the formal structures of the propositional calculi of truth-functional and modal logic do not capture the syntax of the laws of nature, what does? In order to answer this, we must first debunk a myth about the laws of nature that follows directly from the above two logical expressions. It has been widely assumed that the laws of nature are universal. If they are true, they hold for all and every kind of entities or phenomena, irrespective of their intrinsic properties. For example, the laws of biology are true of stones because stones are not biological systems. This fact renders the antecedent of the conditionals which allegedly express the biological laws false. And according to the principles of propositional logic a conditional with a false antecedent is true regardless of the truth or falsity of the consequent. We find this sense of universality of laws to be completely indefensible. On the contrary, it is our contention that laws are 'ontologically localised' to specific types of phenomena. Which law applies to a system depends on the location of the type to which that system belongs in the type-hierarchy that expresses the common ontology of a certain field of phenomena. By insisting on this commonsense restriction of the range of application of laws, we are able to avoid the paradoxes of material implication. It was those very paradoxes which permitted the implausible inferences which we highlighted in the problem of cotenability.

Limiting the range of application of a law of nature to things that are of 'the right stuff' would come as no surprise to a scientist (quoted from Aronson, 1989). After all, while the predicate 'has eight electrons orbiting its nucleus' readily applies to atoms, being true of the atoms of oxygen but false of other atoms, no scientist in his right mind would apply such a predicate to bananas, or to the white shoes of the famous raven paradox, for that matter. It just not make sense to ask whether bananas have or have not eight orbital electrons. In the same way Snell's Law covers light refraction while Young's modulus is used to deal with beams of different materials and not *vice versa*. Do Mendel's laws sensibly apply to light rays or ideal gases? Does the ideal gas law automatically hold true of planetary orbits? We do not think that it makes any sense at all to discuss the 'logic' of such laws as these as if they could be applied unproblematically across diverse categories of things without requiring some evidence *that they are really of the same type*. This holds just as much for the ways people apply folk laws. Who in his right mind would apply the proto-law 'The harder you hit something, the further it goes' to mental phenomena? Or to the air?

Following the lead of philosophers such as Dretske (1977), Swoyer (1982), Armstrong (1983) et al., we propose that it is simply wrong to think of laws as applying in any and all conditions. Instead we propose to think of them as expressing contextually and ontologically constrained invariant relationships between properties. For example, Newton's second law says that if a body is endowed with mass, that is, is of the right stuff for the application of Newton's laws of mechanics, the relationship, $F = ma$ applies to it. Of course, it is not just any relationship that holds for the system in question. It must be one that remains invariant under spacetime translations in the actual world. For example, if a body has mass, the relationship embodied in the second law is true of it, no matter where it happens to be located in space and time.

According to the view of laws we are putting forth here, there are two parts to the content of any lawlike statement. On the one hand we have *implicit ontological conditions,* viz. those features an object must have in order for the relationship in question to hold of it and of things of the same type. If a body were not endowed with mass, it would not be of 'the right stuff' for Newton's laws to be applied to it. If we were faced with something blue in colour, it would be of the right type for Newton's laws of optics to apply. But this feature would not warrant the application of Newton's laws of mechanics. No one knew this better than Newton himself! On the other hand, having mass would not, in itself, be enough to justify bringing Maxwell's laws to bear on some problem (cf. Harré, 1973: 367-73).

The second part of the content of lawlike statements includes the relationships among properties which apply to systems that possess the prerequisite ontological features. It is this part of the content of lawlike statements that usually appears explicitly in standard formulations of laws of nature. In physics, we speak of relationships between magnitudes, which are represented as sets of ordered n-tuples, the algebraic functions expressing laws. In contrast to the traditional truth-functional analysis of laws, it is the relationship among magnitudes that carries much of the burden of lawhood, not material implication between the antecedent and consequent clauses of an 'If ... then ... ' statement. So, instead of representing the structure of a law statement as a universal conditional, $(x)(Fx \supset Gx)$, and its content as the predicates 'F' and 'G' we claim that the content of a law statement is best expressed as follows:

A physical system, X, satisfies ontological conditions, $C_1, \ldots, C_n$, and there is a relationship among properties, R, which holds for x.

Instead of a law being formally represented by a relationship between sentences it should be represented by a mapping, f, whose domain is the set of ontological conditions, $C_1, \ldots, C_n$ and whose range is a set of ordered n-tuples $<a1 \ldots an>$. Formally the expression of a law will look something like this:

$$f{:}(C_1, \ldots, C_n) \ \longrightarrow \ \{<a1, a2, \ldots, an>\}.$$

For example, consider Newton's second law, $F = ma$, which applies to mass points and combinations of them. In this case, we have $f: (m) \longrightarrow \{<F,a>\}$, i.e. given that a body has such and such mass various accelerations go with various forces.

5. The consequence approach revised

Suppose a piece of chalk is suspended in a gravitational field. This set-up is of just the right stuff for motion in a gravitational field. In fact the possibilities are infinite but constrained. If released or thrown, the chalk will not turn into a pumpkin, but it could fall straight down, describe a parabolic arch, go straight up and then straight down. It can do anything within a range of possibilities fixed by the ontological conditions for laws of mechanics, and compatible with the laws of motion that hold for that particular circumstance. This means that this state of affairs supports the truth of as many counterfactuals as there are ways of releasing or throwing the chalk. What is of special importance, here, is that the possibilities are all contained in the situation in the same way that, in quantum field theory, the vacuum is assumed to contain the various possibilities of combinations of particles in different states 'bubbling out'.

Now we can explicate modalities in terms of laws as we have characterised them above. We have seen that possibility requires that the event in question is lawlike permissible for a system that satisfies the prerequisite conditions for the said lawlike relationship to apply. For example, to say that the drink can possibly kill you means that it is of the right stuff (it has a certain chemical make-up), such that if it were to enter a biological system of a certain type it would cause that system to cease to function:

P is possible for x if and only if x satisfies $C_1, \ldots, C_n$ of a lawlike relationship, where P is the second (or more) member of one of the n-tuples of the range of f.

Of course, if the drink does not contain any of the right stuff, it cannot possibly poison you, i.e. there is no lawlike relationship between the properties it does have and death.

P is impossible for x if and only if there are no $C_1, \ldots, C_n$ that x satisfies, such that P is the second (or more) member of one of the n-tuples of the range of f.

There is no mention of possible worlds in the above depictions of the concepts of 'possibility' and 'impossibility'.

A corresponding treatment of the concept of 'necessity' naturally follows:

P is necessary for x if and only if x satisfies $C_1, \ldots, C_n$ of a lawlike relationship where P is the second (or more) member of all of the n-tuples of the range of f. No matter what happens to x, P will occur.

For example, the laws of relativity are such that no matter what we do to a material system, its velocity relative any inertial frame will always be less than the velocity of light.

Now consider counterfactuals or contrary-to-fact conditionals. To say, 'If this chalk were released it would fall' means (1) that the situation of the chalk being located in a gravitational field includes being of the right stuff for Newton's laws to apply and (2) that the laws are such that releasing the chalk is coupled with its falling.

In general: If P were the case, Q would have occurred for x if and only if $C_1, \ldots, C_n$ is true of x and there is an f with $C_1, \ldots, C_n$ as its domain while $<P,Q>$ is a member of the range of f.

What we are advocating with this characterisation of counterfactuals is that $<P,Q>$, (P and Q are coupled), is to replace both 'If P is true then Q will be true' and 'If P were to be true then Q would be true'. This is in keeping with the above intuition that there is no real difference in the state of affairs referred to by 'If P is the case then Q is or will be the case' and 'If P were the case then Q would be the case'. It is also clear how using $<P,Q>$ to represent 'If P then Q' avoids the paradoxes of material implication, for it is not truth-functional. Whether $<P,Q>$ is true of or holds for system x depends set-theoretically on whether $<P,Q>$ is a member of the range of f. So, we have avoided the paradoxes of material implication without having to postulate possible worlds.

This does not mean, however, that this analysis rules out any possibility of possible worlds. We shall see that not only does this theory of counterfactuals allow for possible worlds, it also brings in *virtual worlds*. Like Lewis' (1991) position this theory allows for open futures, yielding the following topological picture (Figure 7.1) of counterfactual truths:

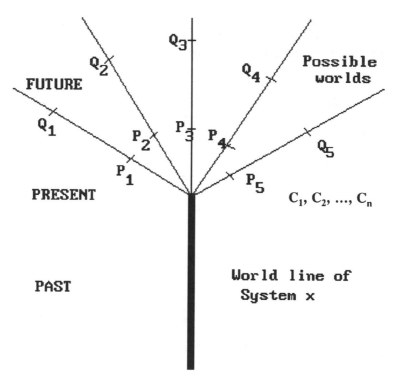

Figure 7.1. A 'picture' of physical possibility

The world line of x is a single line in the past, up to the present. The ontological conditions, $C_1, C_2, \ldots, C_n$, are true of x at the present and in any future time that x might be subject to some physical interaction.

According to the above diagram, x has an open future: that is, there are many possible ways x can evolve, each 'future' being lawlike permissible. In other words, x is of the right stuff for a set of laws apply to it, and so it contains just these future possibilities. There is a one-to-one correspondence between each member of the set of ordered pairs in the range of f and a branch in x's 'future tree'. Each branch of the future tree can be considered a possible world. It cannot be identified with the actual world and it has yet to exist. Notice that the truth of each counterfactual describing the several branches of the future tree is not discovered by making similarity comparisons among branching worlds, as Lewis (1973) and Jackson (1977) would have it. On the contrary, the legitimacy of a branch and hence the truth of the counterfactual describing it, depends on its being generated by f. Possible worlds, then, do not determine the truth of the corresponding counterfactuals. It is the other way around. Which counterfactuals are true tells us which are the possible worlds, relative to the ontological conditions which alone make possible the application of any laws at all.

Except for those who insist on the tenseless view of time, viz. that the past, present and future are equally real and, somehow, all exist – no one should have any difficulty in using the concept of 'possible worlds' without having to postulate their existence or giving them equal status with the actual (present) world. There are many possible worlds stemming from X at this moment – that is, are 'contained' in it – but only one of them *will* exist. None of them exists at present. Counterfactuals about the past can be made sense of simply by requiring that we relativise the 'present' starting point for each of them to some temporal location in the past, where branching is imagined to begin. This treatment is similar to the double indexicality introduced by Reichenbach in his account of more complex tenses. Again, this way of making sense of past counterfactuals does not entail that past possible worlds once existed, any more than the corresponding treatment of future counterfactuals entails the existence of a multiplicity of future possible worlds. That the actual world is 'rich' enough to incorporate possibilities was proposed by Goodman (1965: 57):

> What we often mistake for the actual world is one particular description of it. And what we mistake for possible worlds are just equally true descriptions in other terms. We have come to think

of the actual as one among many possible worlds. We need to repaint that picture. All possible worlds lie within the actual one.

However, unlike Goodman, we insist that such a dispositional picture of possibilities requires that laws are thought of as relations among the properties of any particular system.

6. A recipe or procedure for evaluating counterfactuals

The above depiction of counterfactuals leaves us with this recipe for determining the truth of a counterfactual claim:

In order to evaluate a counterfactual – that is, to decide whether <*P,Q*> holds for a particular system, *x* – there must a 'law of the system' whose variables cover the values of *P* and *Q*. The law(s) of a system depends on what *type* of system *x* happens to be. For example, consider the law of the pendulum. The pendulum is a system which can be subsumed under many different types: harmonic, constrained, gravitational, and so on (see Figure 2.3). Which lawlike relations apply to a given system? That depends on what *type* of system it is. Once that is determined, we can ascertain which laws that hold for the system by seeing what supertypes it falls under. The laws that apply are some of the metaproperties of each supertype and, necessarily, *x* inherits them. We have learned in Chapter Two that the law(s) of the system can then be seen as the combination of these inherited laws into a single law(s). The derivation of the pendulum law

$$T = 2\pi \sqrt{l/g}$$

is a case in point.

The trick, then, for determining the truth of <*P,Q*>, for telling whether it holds or does not hold for the system *x*, is to factor out or isolate the variables that have the physical dimensions of *P* and *Q*. A physicist, such as Galileo, must come up with a law of the system with only two variables which must be of the same dimensions as those picked out by <*P,Q*>. In the case of the pendulum, suppose we wished to evaluate the following counterfactual:

If the length of a pendulum were to increase then its period would increase.

The first step would be to locate the type of system that this pendulum instantiates in a physical type-hierarchy. Then one would combine the various laws that apply to the supertype systems above it in the hierarchy until we derive a law that contains the variables of length and period only. In this case, it is

$$T = 2\pi \sqrt{l/g}$$

just as Galileo concluded.

For counterfactuals of the form 'If P were the case, then Q would be the case', P and Q are respectively independent and dependent variables. So, for the above counterfactual, the values of T are a function of l and not the reverse. Of course, this counterfactual is true. Differentiating the law of the pendulum yields a set of ordered pairs in which an increase of length will always be coupled with an increase of the period.

The counterfactual 'If this chalk were released it would fall' can be treated in the same manner. In this case, we have a piece of chalk and the earth forming a Newtonian system of two spatially separated masses. Combining the law of gravitational attraction with Newton's laws of motion, we can derive a law with only two variables. One refers to how a body is released and the other to its subsequent motion. The chalk is of a type with this type of body. So, via the type identity, these ordered pairs can all be attributed to the chalk. For example, if the chalk is thrown outward, its motion will be parabolic. On the other hand, if it is simply released, it will fall straight down. The ordered pair, <release,fall> is a member of the range of that law.

The match case requires a good deal of imaginative filling in of unknown conditions but the idea is basically the same. The match, the match box, their relationship and the surroundings are a type of physical-chemical system, having a specific location in a physical-chemical type-hierarchy. In other words the match as a system possesses physical and chemical properties in such a way that various physical and chemical laws apply to it, since it inherits these laws from the supertypes under which its type falls. These laws can be combined so that various ways of striking the match and its lighting or not lighting appear as separate variables. The resultant ordered pairs are then attributed to the match, where the first member of each ordered pair denotes a particular way of striking the match and the second member can denote either lighting or not lighting. 'If the match were to be struck *in such and such a way*, it would light' is true if and only if <being struck such and such a way, lighting> is a member of the set of ordered pairs holding for systems of that type.

There is something very striking about the match case. The traditional, deductive nomological way of applying laws to a system is to have the properties of the system serve as initial conditions and to use those laws to link up these conditions with a consequent physical outcome. Instead of dealing with a list of properties, we are first identifying the type of system under investigation, locating it in a type-hierarchy in order to come up with a set of laws for that type of system. Other types of systems will have their own set of distinct laws. This is another way of saying that laws are ontologically relativised. If we really want an answer to 'Would *this* match light if I were to strike it?', we can not think of the match in isolation but as part of a specific type of system. It is not enough simply to list what seem to be the relevant properties. We must think about how they fit together as a specific type of system.

This is why the match case is so complicated and difficult. Most of us, including chemists, do not know the law(s) of systems of such a specific type, as just this match in just this environment. Resorting to possible worlds is no help. How would we know if it is true that in a world very similar to ours the match will light if struck without appealing to the very laws of the system for which we are searching? For those of us who are ignorant of scientific laws and possible worlds, how are we to evaluate counterfactuals?

Although some of the above cases were settled by applying scientific laws, exactly the same strategy is used in ordinary situations, except that the laws the ordinary person uses, folk laws, are not as mathematically precise as those in the natural sciences. Consider 'If that ball had been hit in the stadium in my town it would not have gone so far'. While such a counterfactual is not based upon Newton's laws, it is based on folk laws like 'The harder the ball is hit, the further it will travel' or 'The more the wind blows, the less the ball will travel'. These proto-laws can be combined, along with the fact that there is almost always a strong wind blowing against the batsman in that town, to derive a simple law for the type of the local system, a law that supports the above counterfactual. The same can be said of the match case. Press on the box lightly and the match will not get sufficiently hot; press too firmly and it will break; strike it in the wind and it will blow out; and, so on.

We have seen that, in the match-striking case, even with sophisticated laws, scientists are still confronted with very complex systems. It is at this point that models make their appearance in the physical and engineering sciences. In the earlier chapters, we have demonstrated that a model system is a system that resembles the real system in the relevant way in virtue of their relative locations in a type-hierarchy. The model system and the real system inherit the same supertype laws to the extent that they have the same or similar system laws. They will differ, of course. There is friction at the point of attachment of a real pendulum; its string has mass and is elastic; the gravitational field in which it moves is non-uniform; and its oscillations are dampened by the atmosphere in which it moves. Not so for the model pendulum; unlike the weights that oscillate on strings and chains in such places as the baptistry at Pisa, the pendulums of the real world, it is 'perfect'.

Yet, if the differences between the model system are not relevant or so small as not to count for much, we can use the model system to determine the truth of a counterfactual for the real system. Either we can use the law for the model system to determine its truth, as we did above, or we can directly observe how the model system behaves in a variety of situations. This has its advantages, as we have learned earlier. In general, it is easier, safer and less expensive to test counterfactuals by model manipulation than to work with the real thing. We also know that there are scientific situations where it is impossible to test counterfactuals when it comes to the real system, and that models provide us with a unique kind of virtual world experimentation.

The above use of models to evaluate counterfactuals presupposes a very important metaphysical principle:

> Small differences between the initial conditions of the model system and the real system lead to small divergences in their behaviour.

The nature of the atmosphere is such that our weather system is unstable at each point in the atmosphere. Small differences in initial conditions lead to great divergences in behaviour. According to chaos theory, the above principle is violated. If so, we can not model the weather, for infinitesimal differences between initial conditions of the model system and of the actual atmospheric system will lead to divergent counterfactuals. Using weather models to support counterfactuals about the greenhouse effect is, unfortunately, a risky business if the weather is a chaotic system, in the technical sense.

7. Some comparisons between the approaches

We have already seen how the above analysis of counterfactuals is not based on assumptions about the existence of possible worlds or on comparisons between them in terms of similarity or closeness. We have also seen that while this is not a truth-functional approach, it is non-truth-functional in a way other than the traditional possible world semantics. For example, in each possible world, the truth of 'If P then Q' is still determined truth-functionally while the truth of $<P,Q>$ is not truth-functionally determined in the actual world or any world, possible or otherwise.

Let us examine how the two rival views treat a well-known illustration of the failure of the predicate calculus to handle counterfactuals. Truth-functionally, 'If $(P.R)$ then Q' follows logically from 'If P then Q'. However, from the truth of 'If I were to walk on the ice, it would not break,' we cannot infer 'If I and my pet elephant were to walk on the ice, it would not break'. The possible worlds approach bars this inference by showing that while the former proposition is true there are many possible worlds closely resembling ours (in one of which I am always accompanied by my pet elephant) where it is false. The worlds in which the latter is true are more distant from the actual world than those in which it is false. It is not clear how this can be shown without appealing to laws.

How does our revision of the consequence theory handle this case? In the first place, we need the particular law(s) of the type of system in which a weight is placed on ice. Think of the ice as a molecular lattice, write down the Young's modulus (which is a measure of its rigidity) for the ice and arrive at some functional relationship between the forces exerted on this lattice and its structural integrity. Crudely, we can divide the counterfactuals following from such an equation into two sets, one set dealing with forces equal to or greater than some number n while the other set involves forces less than n. If the force in question is equal to or greater than n, the molecular structure fails, that is the ice breaks, but it does not break when the force is less than n. Again, the ontological conditions, which include ice having a certain molecular structure, that structure having a particular Young's modulus, and so on, are the same for each member of the set of ordered pairs of values of the relevant variables in the range of the law which connects breaking or not breaking with different applied forces. So, my walking on the ice, when translated into a body of such and such a mass exerting a force on this lattice, which is less than n, supports 'If I were to walk on the ice, it would not break.' However, *the very same law and the same ontological conditions also support* 'If I and my pet elephant were to walk on the ice it would break.' The truth of these two counterfactuals stem from the same law and conditions. '<F = 185, no break>' and '<F = 2185, break>' are both members of the range of Young's modulus law.

How is cotenability handled by each analysis? Lewis' position claims to do what Goodman insisted could not be done, namely independently to establish the truth of a counterfactual that guarantees the enabling conditions will hold once the antecedent of the conditional occurs:

Say that x is cotenable with an entertainable antecedent ϕ at a world i if and only if x holds throughout some ϕ permitting sphere around i; say also that x is cotenable with ϕ at i if x holds throughout every sphere around i whether or not ϕ is entertainable (Lewis, 1979: 69).

This is a strong sense of cotenability, as Lewis admits:

> On my definition, a cotenable premise is not only true, but also necessary to some extent (ibid.: 70).

On this view a cotenable condition can coexist with the occurrence of the antecedent because it must coexist with it.

We find this solution troubling because cotenability is not a relation of necessity but only of compatibility. Why must the truth of ϕ guarantee the truth of x when all we want to establish is the weaker claim that ϕ is compatible with x? Why must there be a necessary connection between ϕ and x? Besides does not Lewis' way of solving the problem play right into Goodman's hands since he uses one counterfactual to support another? Can Lewis find some way to escape the charge that this is a vicious regress?

For us, cotenability is not a question of modalities and possible worlds but one of lawlike independence. To say that the enabling conditions are cotenable with the antecedent of a counterfactual means that they are independent phenomena: that is, there are no lawlike connections between the existence of the enabling conditions and the existence of the antecedent. In particular, there are no lawlike connections between the existence of the antecedent and the non-existence of one or more of the enabling conditions. Let us see how this works.

We have seen that, according to the possible worlds account, cotenability is expressed as a conjunction of an enabling condition premise with the antecedent, such that the consequent is entailed in the nearest worlds. The beauty of our way of representing counterfactuals is that there is a clear-cut distinction between enabling conditions and antecedents: the former are on one side of the mapping while the latter show up as first members of ordered pairs in the range of f. They cannot be conjoined, and they do not have to be in order for the truth of the counterfactual in question to be decided. It simply depends on whether $\langle P,Q \rangle$ is a member of the range set. So, this answers Goodman's version of the cotenability problem, for any truth-functional deduction of the denial of one of the conditions when the antecedent is true is blocked once laws are properly expressed in terms of the above mapping.

Another nice feature of our analysis is that our expressions for laws contain enough information to tell us in a non-*ad hoc* way when we have cotenability and when we do not. This is because natural laws have time parameters to allow for the fact that the occurrence of the antecedent may change the enabling conditions *at the time* of their occurrence. In this case they are not lawlike independent. But this information can be easily handled by our mapping functions. Since the cotenability and non-cotenability information occur in the range of *f* they are equally compatible with the enabling conditions.

Consider this imaginary example to illustrate what is meant by the above. Suppose we wish counterfactually to describe the motion of a body, *a*, were it to be released in a peculiar type of force field. Let us say that the laws for this system tell us that *a* moves along a field line or geodesic. Before it is released, the field lines are perfectly straight. So, we could deduce that when *a* is released, it will move in a straight line. Now add the assumption that the act of releasing *a* in the field causes field lines to bend. How, then, can we show that 'If *a* were released in these conditions, it would move in a straight line' is false while 'If *a* were released in these conditions, it would move along a curve' is true, even though the lines of the field are perfectly straight before *a* is released? According to our strategy, the solution involves recognising that there is a lawlike relationship between *how* the lines of the field warp as a function of how objects are released. The information about a suspended *a* and a rectilinear field is contained in the domain of *f* while the information about the lines of the field and *a*'s motion as a function of releasing *a* in various ways is packed into the range of *f*. It should be clear that there are no contradictions here, no cotenability problems. So, we have yet another good reason to replace the 'If *P* then *Q*' formulation with '<*P,Q*>'.

The backtracking version of the cotenability problem can be handled in essentially the same way. Will a past that leads to the occurrence of the antecedent also lead to the demise of one of the enabling conditions? According to our view, this amounts to asking if there is a lawlike connection between the past in question which leads to the antecedent and the demise of the enabling conditions. The reason why we relativise the question to particular pasts is that, obviously, some pasts will be cotenable while others will not be. The point is that the pasts of some systems being lawlike independent of the future of others is perfectly compatible with determinism. All determinism claims is that the laws of nature are such that the initial state of the universe determines one and only one future. It does not claim that any one *part* of the universe must affect the future states of all the other parts. For example, we could easily imagine a Leibnizian universe consisting only of non-interacting bodies. The future state of each body is completely determined by its past; and so, for the future state of the entire universe. Even so, because this deterministic universe consists of nothing but monads, any past is cotenable with any future.

Laws describing the time lines of many-bodied systems are very complex and, indeed, difficult if not impossible to discover. However, this is an epistemic problem, not a semantic one, and the cotenability problem is one of semantics. If, as a matter of fact, not of knowledge, the past in question is lawlike independent of the enabling conditions, we have cotenability. For example, in the match case, there are many ways in which a match can be brought into contact with the box that will not affect the presence of oxygen. On the other hand, moving it up at one hundred kilometres per hour might cause a partial vacuum, removing the oxygen. That past is not cotenable.

8. Virtual worlds versus possible worlds

It is important to realise that possible worlds cannot possibly play the same role in scientific realism that normal theoretical entities play. Modal realism may seem like traditional scientific realism but it is not at all like that because possible worlds are not open to empirical considerations. In the first place, modal realism says that similarity between co-existing possible worlds determines the semantics of modal propositions. For example, even though a proposition may be false in the actual world, it is possibly true if it is true in one of those worlds sufficiently nearest (similar) to the actual world. In contrast to this, our version of possibility is determined by lawlike permissibility, i.e. the generation of a virtual world state is a function of the laws governing the system under investigation.

A sincere modal realist claims that the existence of possible worlds, which are related by accessibility, must be postulated if we are in any way to make sense of the truth or falsity of modal propositions. So, it almost looks as though we are positing possible worlds in the same way Newton postulated absolute space and time or the way scientists normally posit the existence of any highly theoretical entity. Not so, if we think about it, for there are glaring differences between the two types of realism. For example, while Newton admitted that absolute space could not be observed directly, its effects on motion could be detected. The same could be said for any theoretical entity: its effects should, in principle, be observable. Something should count as evidence for or against its existence, i.e. it should leave its mark in the actual world.

But how could the existence or non-existence of possible worlds, as they are depicted by the modal realist, make their effects known in the actual world, thereby generating evidence? Such evidence is impossible, for the existence or non-existence of possible worlds only 'affects' the truth values of modal propositions, something we cannot possibly observe. Besides, according to the modal realist, their truth values cannot be determined independently of possible worlds. So, possible worlds may come and go, but we have no way of learning about this by observing the actual world.

In contrast to this, because the laws that generate virtual worlds are open to empirical considerations, our version of modal actualism is perfectly entrenched in traditional scientific realism, especially because it is based on an ordering of natural kinds in the actual world. However, something we share with the modal realist is that modal claims should be objective in the sense that 'their truth is not determined by human convention or human knowledge' (Mondadori & Morton, 1979: 236). In order to avoid being ontologically committed to possible worlds of Lewis' ilk, many versions of modal actualism reduce possibilities to mental constructs or sets of propositions, neither of which are to be found in a mind-independent nature. Like Mondadori and Morton, we have attempted to come up with an analysis of counterfactuals that renders them objective, without having to accept the 'poisoned pawn' of modal realism. The way we have done this is to adopt their (and Goodman's) strategy of treating possibilities as dispositional properties of those things in the actual world that are of the right stuff. Obviously, we do not believe that talk of dispositions can do the job alone. They must be incorporated into our above analysis of laws. Since modal properties are constrained by the laws of nature, they are objective or 'out there', as invariant relationships predicated of systems, whether or not anyone is aware of them. So, modal claims are objective.

As we have stated above, if there are possible worlds, they are harmless as 'branching' futures stemming from the present. Again, the open future is constrained by the laws of the system.

In spite of all our differences, there are similarities between the two approaches. In section 5 and in earlier chapters, we have shown how models play an indispensable role in counterfactual 'experimentation'. If the laws of the real system are not available to us, we take the next best thing by working with a model instead. So we too are making similarity comparisons, but not between possible worlds. We are simply comparing one chunk of the real world, the real system, with a model, which may or may not exist physically. Good working models are often built in the imagination of scientists. From the earlier chapters, we know how these comparisons are to be made. What is particularly important, here, is that similarity comparisons can be made without having to postulate the physical existence of the model system. All we need do is locate the type of the mythological or imaginary model system in the type-hierarchy and apply the Tversky formula accordingly.

The model system can even appear on a computer display, or visually appear to a person through the use of instruments. The latter gives the viewer the illusion of actually living in such a world, in such a way that he is actually observing the truth of a counterfactual: that is, provided that these visualisations are based on the proper laws. So, we can think of these virtual worlds as mini possible worlds that are accessible from the actual world; and we do compare them to a system in the actual world. In fact we do our utmost to make them as similar as possible to the actual system.

While these virtual worlds play an important and, in some cases, an indispensable role in evaluating and visualising possibilities and counterfactuals, they need not exist but if they do they exist in the actual world. So, in this sense, they are not at all like Lewis' possible worlds. However, since virtual worlds are types of systems, they are more than sets of propositions, as some interpreters of possible worlds suggest. But if virtual worlds are in the actual world, it appears that the above revision of the consequence analysis leaves no room for possible worlds in the tendentious Lewis sense.

9. Modal verisimilitude

It is difficult enough to come up with a semantics of verisimilitude and we have seen how establishing a semantics for modalities is rife with problems but there is very little if anything on developing a semantics of truth approximation when it comes to modal propositions. One reason why this is so is that past treatments of these two problems had little or nothing in common. Yet it should be clear that some false counterfactuals are closer to the truth than others. Consider a laboratory pendulum 100 centimetres long. One may use the law of a simple pendulum to support this counterfactual: if the length of the pendulum were to be shortened to 25 centimetres its period would be halved. Of course this counterfactual must be false because the laboratory pendulum can never be a simple pendulum. Nevertheless, although false, this counterfactual is closer to the truth than one which claims the period will double.

How can we rank counterfactual and other modal claims in order of verisimilitude? We have learned that the content of possible, necessary and counterfactual propositions are to be represented in terms of ordered pairs in the range of a mapping, *f*. Another way we have put this is to come up with a model system which resembles the actual system as closely as possible. If the counterfactual is a member of the range of the law for that system, it is true. In the last chapter, we learned that approximate truth was a matter of similarity between a model and the real system, determined by their relative positions in a type-hierarchy, the relative importance of the nodes in the hierarchy, and the Tversky formula. Combining these two sets of principles, we have the following semantics for modalities: the verisimilitude of a modal proposition is a function of how closely the system upon which the modal claim is based resembles the actual system, and how similar the laws of the model system are to the actual system. How closely a model resembles the real system and how closely their laws resemble each other depends on how they are interrelated in the relevant type-hierarchy.

If the counterfactual is based on a model system that is of exactly the same type and dimensions as the real system, this counterfactual is simply true, our limiting case again. If the difference between the two systems leads to a divergence in behaviour that is nevertheless within the limits of the scope of the claim, it is still true. For example, in the above case, if one simply claimed that shortening the length of the laboratory pendulum would decrease its period, even though such a claim is based on a model (simple pendulum), it is still true. Again all this depends on accepting the anti-chaos assumption.

The incorporation of modalities and verisimilitude now completes the unification of the important doctrines of realism, something the traditional treatment of theories, models, verisimilitude, truth and modalities could not do.

CHAPTER EIGHT

A Realist Theory of Properties

1. Properties in physics: the primary and secondary quality distinction

It is not too much to say that the science of physics took its great leap forward in the seventeenth century as much from the new metaphysics of properties as from the successful development of mathematical representations of physical processes. Both had been foreshadowed in earlier periods, but in the hands of Bacon, Galileo, Newton and Boyle the twin pillars of modern physics, its metaphysics and its method, were fully developed. We will begin with a brief sketch of the history of the primary and secondary quality distinction.

The physical sciences, since antiquity, had made use of the Parmenidean principle that the world as it appears to a human observer is different from the world as it really is. The philosophical problems implicit in this seemingly simple distinction are still with us, in particular the problem of giving an adequate account of the meaning of that potent phrase 'as it really is', and to justify the use of the distinction between appearance and reality that it facilitates. The bulk of this book has been devoted to developing just such an account. What then are physical properties?

Bacon was among the first to grasp the significance of the atomic hypothesis for a theory of properties. The thesis that the physical world really is a swarm of mobile atoms requires a contrast between observed phenomena, which are not generally of that kind, and the corresponding states and processes in nature which are. What is the nature of this correspondence? Bacon's analysis of physical properties into manifest natures and 'latent processes and configurations' and the examples he used to illustrate it made the form of the Parmenidean duality of modern physics clear. But the logical grammar, so to say, that

was needed to develop the metaphysics of the distinction came
later. He illustrated the need for the introduction of hypotheses
about latent processes into physics with examples such as this:
'fire' is the cause of 'colliquation' when applied to wax, but of
'induration' when applied to clay. There must be something
about the several natures of wax and of clay that accounts for
the difference. Nothing that appears to the naked eye could play
that role, so there must be distinctive latent properties, properties Gassendi was later to call *occultae*.

It was in the writings of Locke, Boyle and Newton that the
groundwork of a coherent philosophical theory of the distinctive
character of the 'appearance and reality' metaphysics developed.
In Locke's (1690 [1961]) version a sharp distinction between
ideas (as mental contents) and *qualities* (as attributes of material substances) permeates his whole treatment. The pri-
mary/secondary distinction orders both ideas and qualities into
matching sets. In the universe of ideas those that are of secondary qualities are distinguished by their variability with the
condition of the human observer, a criterion that was central to
Galileo's treatment of the distinction. In *Il saggiatore* he uses
the contrast between the effect of a mechanical stimulation on
the body of a man and of a statue, to distinguish 'mechanical'
from 'sensible' qualities. The latter exists only by virtue of
human sensibility; the former by virtue of the materiality of both
bodies. The weakness of the 'variability' criterion has been
obvious from the beginning. All perceived qualities of bodies can,
in the appropriate circumstances, vary with the condition and
location of the observer. The warmth, colour, taste and so on of
material things and substances, considered as they were expe-
rienced, were classified as ideas of secondary qualities. 'Bulk,
figure, texture [configuration of parts] and motion', to use
Boyle's well-known catalogue, were distinguished as ideas of
primary qualities.

However, a glance at these lists reveals another and more
radical distinction. The ideas of secondary qualities do not
suggest an atomic or corpuscularian ontology. They do not reveal
themselves as attributes of systems of particles in motion. The
ideas of primary qualities clearly do. If the world, in general, is
taken to be corpuscularian, a swarm of mobile particles, cluster-
ing, separating and reforming, then a second, more robust

criterion for distinguishing one class of ideas from another emerges. Only the ideas of primary qualities resemble the actual qualities of material beings, as these are determined by the corpuscularian ontology. Generations of scholars have found the philosophy of science of Locke and Boyle wanting at just this point. How could we ever know that the criterion of resemblance had been met, since, as human beings, we know nothing but ideas? But this, we believe, is the result of a misunderstanding of the structure of their account. It is not inductive. It is not that Locke and Boyle asked themselves 'What could material stuff really be like?' and looked for an answer by generalising a distinction among ideas. Rather it is hypothetico-deductive. What if the world were indeed corpuscularian? What would that hypothesis tell us about our human ideas? In our terminology, Locke and Boyle are proposing a 'common ontology', echoed by Newton, for the accomplishment of the programme of physical science.

In the light of the assumption of an ontology of corpuscles, what are we to make of the fact that there are many ideas of qualities which are patently non-corpuscularian? It is here that Locke's great metaphysical innovation appears. However, these ideas might seem, in the material body which manifests them, they can only be matched by *powers*. To say that something is coloured such and such a hue, is to ascribe to that thing a power to produce just that idea in the conscious experience of a human observer. How does it come about that material things and substances have these powers? It is because of the specific arrangement of their corpuscular structure, in Boyle's terminology, their 'texture'. We shall adopt the following terminology in our development of this potent philosophical theory: 'Powers are *grounded* in the *natures* of things and substances.' The natures of things and substances are what physicists, in terms of their working common ontology, tell us of the constitution of those things and material substances.

All these concepts will need further development. However, at this point one further historical observation is necessary. The obvious question to pose to Locke and Boyle is this: if secondary qualities are nothing but powers to produce certain ideas (perceptual experiences) why should we not make the same point about primary qualities? This innovation was picked up very quickly. Beginning with Greene (1727) a philosophy of physics developed, particularly in England, based on a generalisation of the 'powers' ontology. Material corpuscles were swept away in favour of real powers. The same idea took root somewhat later in continental Europe. It was used by R.J. Boscovich (1763) in his famous attempt to reconcile the ontologies of Newton and Leibniz. It was developed in characteristic detail by Kant (1786 [1970]). It was the target of Hume's sceptical criticism in both his *Treatise* (1739) and his *Enquiry* (1748).

2. The conditionality of properties I: simple dispositions

The theory of properties we shall be developing is a linear descendent of the property metaphysics of the eighteenth century as it grew out of critical appraisals of the philosophy of physics of Locke and Boyle. Our object is to expound a philosophical grammar for the property concepts of physical science that will complete the argument of the whole book. Once again the basic working concepts of our formal treatment of the content of physical thought will be 'conditionality' and 'type-hierarchy'. And our basic working concepts for expressing that content will be 'model' and 'natural kind'.

In our view even the simplest seeming property concept is internally complex. To say that something is heavy is not only to refer to experiences or the responses of instruments should we or they encounter it, but it is to ascribe to that entity some permanent state which, if the thing interacts (were to interact) with people or instruments, will (would) manifest itself as weight. The concept of 'heaviness' then is internally complex. Its structure includes a conditional element and a categorical element. After much tortuous conceptual twisting and turning by the late seventeenth century the concept of 'mass' had emerged as the categorical element in heaviness attributions, while 'weight' did duty for the phenomena expected on the fulfilment of the appropriate conditions. In many ways this treatment preserves the main insights of Locke and Boyle, generalised as metaphysics for all kinds of properties. The conditional element we shall refer to as the 'dispositional' component and the categorical element as its 'grounding'. By the end of the nineteenth

century Mach had realised that these concepts formed a hierarchy, in that 'mass' too was best analysed as a dispositional
concept, grounded in some macro-property of the universe as a
whole.

The general form of a property-as-power attribution looks
something like this:

$$\text{If } C \text{ then } B \text{ by virtue of } N$$

where 'C' represents the conditions for the manifestation of
behaviour 'B', by entities whose physical nature is 'N'. In general
our knowledge of what 'N' is, in any given case, is derived from
theorising on the basis of the current common ontology, in the
manner we have analysed in preceding chapters. The 'N' concept
in some scientific discourse refers, so we have argued, to a model
of the physical nature of the entity in question. It follows that
all property attributions, when analysed, *have the form of
theories*.

Our treatment of properties permits another slant on the
progressivism we are defending. Property attributions in physics and chemistry can be displayed as hierarchies. Let us suppose that the properties that are under investigation in a
laboratory are those we loosely call the 'strength of materials'.
Tensile strength and deformations of rods, let us say, under
tension, can be expressed in just such a form as that above. The
'Ns' first cited in grounding the mechanical dispositions of different materials are molecular structures. However, the component molecules of those structures play the roles they do because
they possess certain properties, the analysis of which will take
the same form. The 'Ns' cited in this level of physics will be the
internal structures of molecules, their atomic architecture, so to
say. The atomic constituents of these structures have properties
which can be – indeed, if it is physics we are embarked upon –
must be treated in the same way, and so on. Let us call this
procedure 'attribute stripping'. There are many attribute-strip-
ping regresses being constructed by physical scientists, each of
which regresses towards the same common ontology, the ontology of the general physics of the era. It is pertinent to remind
ourselves that in this case, just as in the case of the primitive
version of this theory of properties proposed by Locke and Boyle,

it is a mistake to think that the '*Ns*' are simple empirical discoveries, like coming across Easter Island. We are constructing models of the natures of things, based on a type-hierarchy which expresses our common ontology. The question of how to tell whether the models resemble the real natures of things is another question. To borrow an expression from J.M. Saguillo, our enterprise is ontosemantic, not epistemological. We have already advanced a theory of the ontosemantics of conditionality in Chapter Seven. With this sketch of the ontosemantics of groundings the outline of our theory of properties is complete. However, in filling in the details some very important additions must be made.

Failure to follow through with the dispositionalist theory of physical properties can have unwelcome consequences. For instance, Eddington (1929), starting from a version of the primary and secondary quality distinction, gave an account of the relation between the grounding state and the display of a disposition based on his notorious ontology of the 'two tables'. One existed in the world of human experience, the other in the world of physics, and they were duplicates of one another. These worlds were causally related. We cannot do better than quote Stebbing's (1937) diagnosis of the source of Eddington's position. 'Eddington takes quite seriously,' she says, 'the view that there are *two tables*; ... Eddington's philosophy may be regarded as the outcome of a sustained attempt to answer the question: How are the two tables related to one another? ... In answering the question he is hampered by his initial assumption that the tables are *duplicates* of each other ... .' On the dispositionalist view there is just the one table. Considered as a whole, it has certain dispositions, for instance to be seen table-like by a person-world ensemble. Those and other dispositions are grounded in the physical structure of the table as it is represented in the best working model. Eddington has construed the ontology of the disposition-grounding pair in terms of substances. In much the same way Descartes ended up with a two-substance ontology for human beings.

3. The conditionality of properties II: complex dispositions

The general drift of Bohr's philosophy of physics is clear enough in hindsight (Honner, 1987). It is also clear that his contemporaries, in particular Einstein, did not understand Bohr's position at all. Einstein's assumption that Bohr was advocating some kind of positivistic, Berkleyan interpretation of physics (Schillp, 1949) shows just how wide of the mark was his grasp of Bohr's notion of the 'phenomenon'. Einstein and Bohr are not opposed as realist and positivist, but as absolutist and relationist. ('Relationism' is emphatically not 'relativism', this confusion leading to yet other mistaken readings of Bohr.) Einstein believed that it was possible to give an objective and absolutist characterisation of material reality, from which the actual results of experimental manipulations could be deleted, the apparatus serving simply to fix and locate the independent properties and processes of material reality. Bohr saw that the performing of an experiment created an 'internal' relation between the material apparatus as used by the experimenter and the material stuff with which it interacted. The relation is 'internal' in that the apparatus, when in use, brings into being a state of affairs which, though it is the manifestation of a real disposition or tendency or natural power of the world stuff, is not just a manifestation of those dispositions. The form that manifestation takes is shaped by the apparatus and the way it is used. The indissoluble totality of apparatus-world manifestation is what Bohr meant by a phenomenon. It makes no sense to ask 'What would an electron be like if there were no electron-displaying apparatus?' since the world disposition in question is only displayed *as an electron* in that kind of set-up. There is nothing subjectivist or relativist about this idea. 'Electrons' are relational properties of some well-defined types of apparatus-world ensembles.

What can we ascribe as a property? Conveniently a new kind of dispositional concept was introduced into the psychology of perception for a class of properties of which Bohrian phenomena seem clearly to be a subclass. Gibson (1979) called them 'affordances' and we shall borrow this terminology. We shall say,

expressing the ontosemantics of the Bohrian 'phenomena' talk,
that a certain kind of apparatus-world ensemble *affords* the
relevant category of entities, properties, processes and so on
to some instrument or observer or manipulator. Ontologically
these are one and all properties of the apparatus-world
ensemble.

An experimental observation is the result of paying attention
to the state of an apparatus that is displaying whatever effect
the set-up has power or tendency to produce. Positivists would
say that what is displayed is a disposition of the observer-appa-
ratus nexus; realists of the Einstein stripe would say that what
is displayed is a disposition of the world independent of the
apparatus, which must be made, so to say, transparent. Rela-
tionists in the Bohr camp would say that what is displayed by
the apparatus is an affordance of the apparatus-world nexus,
which is a complex material entity existing and running independently of human cognition, though it was human beings who
built it and switched it on.

Expressed in the traditional shape of a conditional statement
the logical form of a dispositional ascription looks something like
this:

If a is subjected to X then it manifests Y by virtue of its
physical structure.

In the special case of the Bohrian affordance a denotes a complex
entity of the apparatus-world ensemble type, and X and Y are
treatments and responses that must be able to be expressed in
the language of classical physics. One must be able to manipulate the apparatus and to see or hear what its response is. The
principle of complementarity imposes rigid restrictions on what
treatments can simultaneously be applied to a certain class of
apparatus-world ensembles, namely those which constitute the
repertoire of kinds of apparatus in use in particle physics.

The property ascribed to a by the assertion of the conditional
proposition 'If a is subjected to X then a will manifest Y by virtue
of its physical structure' is just one property of a. It is what
nature (which includes the apparatus!) affords in the conditions
of the experiment. It is a property of the complex but singular
object, the individual apparatus-world ensemble, considered as

an instance of the appropriate type. Clearly this is a relational property, but the relation is internal since the terms 'apparatus' and 'world' cannot be separated *for the purpose of the ascription of physical properties*. The material individuals to which physical properties are ascribed in physical science are just apparatus-world entities. However, the apparatus-world ensemble must be in some determinate state to afford a determinate display of, say, tracks. It is for the representation of this grounding state that we have recourse to models. In the absence of the kind of ontological constraint we shall be discussing in the last section of this chapter exotic models with which to represent the type of the relevant grounding state can flourish. The relevant state of the apparatus-world ensemble might be pictured as a psi-wave collapsing, or as an axial projection of a vector in Hilbert space, and so on.

This is a very sophisticated conception of the ontosemantics of the discourse of physical science. It is scarcely to be wondered at that Einstein, and many others, misunderstood it at the time, expressed as it was in the cloudy rhetoric of the Danish sage. The point is entirely general. For the purposes of the Registrar of births, deaths and marriages, husband-and-wife constitute a singular individual with respect to the internal property 'married'. For an ontology which takes the basic particulars to be individual human beings the predicate 'married' can have no application. It is a predicate only of ensembles.

4. The ontosemantics of three new physical properties

To trace out the complex semantic framework through which the concepts we shall be using to illustrate our analysis have acquired their working meanings, it will be helpful to follow their development, their etymology, if you will. Each has passed through a sequence of meaning stages. The sequence begins with an initial or *original* meaning established by reference to an ultimately dispensable and often visualisable model of the subatomic state of the being which is said to possess the property in question. This state serves to ground a certain disposition which is manifested in well-defined experimental conditions. The sequence ends with the primary model leached out to leave the bare bones of a mathematical structure, such as a correlated pair of vectors, one circulating and the other polar, grounding the same disposition. In this semantic framework we shall say that the concept has a *final* meaning.

The well-known property of *spin* was introduced to explain the phenomenon of the splitting of some spectral lines. The original meaning was created in the semantic framework of Bohr's first atomic model, in which the orbiting electron produced a magnetic field. If the planetary electron was also spinning on an axis normal to the plane of its orbit, then if the spin was in an 'up' sense the magnetic field of the whole atom would be augmented. But if it was oriented in the opposite sense then the magnetic field of the whole atom would be diminished. In this way the phenomenon, an affordance of an apparatus-world ensemble, could be explained. There was quantisation 'in the Z direction', since there could only be two states, spin up or spin down. The final meaning of 'spin' was arrived at by generalising the concept to all subatomic particles, as just one of the quantum states. The effect of this is to dissolve or leach out the model with which the original sense was determined. Certain formal properties implicit in the sense of the original concept remain, for example, that of a polar vector. There are interesting survivals of the original momentum into the final meaning momentum. Physicists do talk of the 'intrinsic angular momentum' of photons. This concept too must be treated as having a final meaning, given by the abstract semantic framework and the surviving cluster of dispositions.

Our second example is a little more exotic, the property of *strangeness*. Like spin, strangeness was to be a property of subatomic particles which could be used to explain some of their dispositions: that is, as a grounding. The new property was introduced by Gell-Mann and Nishijima to account for anomalous or 'strange' behaviour of 'hyperons' and 'kaons'. The decay times for these particles, as measured by the length of their ionisation tracks, were appropriate to particles produced in weak interactions. But these phenomena were the result of strong interactions. There was something strange about these particles, a new property, so why not call it 'strangeness'? This anecdote is amusing, but what was the original model? It was clearly the property of charge. This becomes clear in the formal definition of 'strangeness', 'S'.

$$Q = e(I^3 + (B + S)/2)$$

Since Q and e are both charge concepts S must be understood as a concept like B, baryon number, that is the factor by which the charge on a particle is related to its baryon number. In the new scheme the charge on a particle will be related to its baryon number and its strangeness. Once again the process of abstraction is resorted to and we are left with an abstract grounding of the apparatus-specific dispositions of these classes of particles – that is, of their affordances – with respect to the length, density and curvature of observed tracks.

Yet more exotic to the layperson is our third illustration, the property 'colour'. The original meaning is derived from a model. The model in question is the three-quark architecture of hadrons. No two fermions in the same system can have identical quantum numbers, so somehow the three quarks must be differentiated. 'Colour' behaves like a species of charge. Unlike our other examples, in which the affordances of the apparatus-world ensembles were known and the models constructed and then abstracted to produce the essentially formal or mathematically expressed property, 'colour' began and has remained a formal device for expressing the non-identity of three quarks.

5. Properties in quantum field theory: type-hierarchies again

At this late stage in the argument a familiar concept must be introduced and our version of it explained. That is the concept of 'reference'. In our shift away from a method of analysis that gives priority to the propositional means of knowledge representation there are implications for the whole of the traditional conceptual apparatus of philosophical logic. Reference, at least since Frege's writing on the topic, has been taken to be a relation between words and things. It is treated as an intimate part of the correspondence theory. It has been taken to be more or less the same relation as denotation. Following Roberts (1986) we shall take 'referring' as something people do. An act of reference occurs when someone establishes a physical relation between themselves and some material entity. This can be done with the help of words, but, as Wittgenstein demonstrated in the *Philosophical Investigations*, there are other means available in everyday life. Of the possible physical relations that a person could establish to a material entity the possibility of physical science depends, we suggest, mainly on two – perception and manipulation. Philosophers have long had a tendency to privilege the eye over the hand. This tendency is evident in the way that philosophy of science has focused on the contrast between observable and unobservable realms of being, neglecting the possibilities of manipulation.

Manipulation is a reciprocal relation between person and thing. A person manipulates and a thing reacts to the manipulation. That reaction must terminate in the person again if it is to be relevant to the expansion of scientific knowledge. Experimental physics depends very little on establishing perceptual relations to the entities of the common ontology. It is the possibilities of manipulation that matter. One might be tempted to enunciate a general principle governing manipulative acts, that for each class of manipulations the physical world should display a class of reactions. However, as Curwain has pointed out, there is no *a priori* reason why the manipulations that form a class under some initial classification should be found reliably to evoke a corresponding class of similar responses. Why is this important to us? Generally it is through manipulations and the responses to them that we discover the dispositional properties of our material world. Eventually, as we have shown, the objects of manipulation are confined to those crucial semi-artifacts, the apparatus-world ensembles that appear in laboratories and observatories where the farther reaches of physics are practised.

The concept of a quantised field was made possible through the invention of an ingenious and powerful model. The classical field is thought of in terms of charged entities mutually and continuously interacting by virtue of their spatially distributed field potentials, which represent the energy of the field at each and every point. How should discontinuous or quantised fields be represented? In quantum field theory interactions are pictured as the exchange of discrete particles. The pictures are the Feynman diagrams (Figure 8.1).

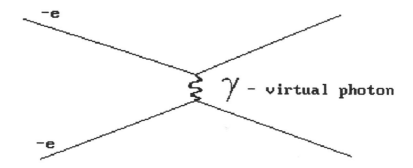

Figure 8.1. A Feynman diagram

There is no place for the 'field' of Faraday and Maxwell in this picture. How seriously should the model be taken? In other words is this picture an amusing metaphor or should it be treated as ontologically significant? That it now has at least some ontological significance is clear from the current literature (Brown and Harré, 1990). One of the reasons is the important role played by the exchange model in the formulation and development of the program of research that culminated in the discovery of W and S particles. In making sense of the story of the exchange model all our major conceptual innovations will play an indispensable part, making it an ideal example with which to round off and summarise the point of view we have been advocating in this book. The old philosophy of science would have been confined to notions like 'observation', 'hypothetico-deductive theory' and 'denotation of terms' in giving an account of this part of physics. Analysed in these terms the story of quantum field theory and the experimental researches it led to is barely intelligible. However, when it is analysed in terms of such concepts as 'model', 'type-hierarchy' and 'manipulation', with the Bohrian concept of 'phenomenon' playing an indispensable role, quantum field theory appears as a triumph of scientific rationality.

The Bohrian scheme consists of two major concepts: 'phenomena' appear as the observable states of individual apparatus-world ensembles. Each type of such ensemble affords, under a certain class of manipulations, a certain type of phenomenon. The properties corresponding to phenomena are therefore 'affordances'. In general in the physical sciences a disposition is assumed to be grounded in a persisting state or process in the material entity having the disposition. Our knowledge of that persisting state is usually indirect and takes the form of a model. At first glance this pattern seems to be repeated in the case of quantum field theory, where the underlying process is, it seems, pictured in the exchange model. The matter will turn out to be a great deal more subtle.

There is something odd about the status of the pictures. The particle-exchange model was introduced by Feynman as a way of displaying the complex conservation relations that must hold in any interaction between subatomic particles. At first sight his diagrams seem very like the familiar photographs of the tracks of interacting particles. But these photographs are in real space and the tracks they picture were made by 'something' in real time. The Feynman diagram is a map in momentum space, the dimensions of which are momentum and time. They do not picture where a particle has been in real space but what its momentum has been. For any given type of particle pair, there are indefinitely many 'diagrams', each picturing one of the set of interactions allowed by quantum mechanics. Is something which is depicted as of the particle-type in momentum space also of the particle-type in real space? In classical mechanics it usually is, since Newtonian bodies have momentum, position and temporal endurance. It is not so clear that the transformation to real space for the 'beings' of quantum field theory preserves ontological type.

To resolve this puzzle we need to take a much closer look at the sources of the particulate model. The tendency among physicists to turn to a particle ontology for the model engendering supertype is not a hangover from atomism. It is to be explained, we believe, by the characteristics of the experimental domain of subatomic physics. The typical result of an experimental manipulation is a *track*. By adjusting the fields to manipulate the unobservable track-producing 'somethings' the end result is a line of droplets, condensing on ionised molecules, or rows of silver atoms or something of the sort. The clicks in Geiger counters and the scintillations on screens are also discrete. The concepts of 'track' and of 'charged particle' mutually support one another. We will call the tracks of such particles 'primary tracks'.

Ian Aitchison has pointed out to us that the relation between the 'track' concept and the 'particle' concept as applied in the context of 'neutral particle' must be more complex. Neutral particles leave no tracks. The use of particulate concepts for the physics of the phenomena for which an ontology of neutral particles is invoked expresses an overt interpretation of the dynamics of those phenomena. However, we believe that this conceptual choice rests in the end on a link with experimentally induced tracks. In studying the photoelectric effect and the Compton effect tracks are observed, and physicists work back from these, using the rule we have articulated above for the interpretation of primary tracks. In this way definite kinematic and dynamic ascriptions are made to the causal predecessors of the track producers. Their direction and momentum ('particle' attributes) can be inferred from the direction and momentum of the successor particles, revealed in tracks. We shall call these tracks 'secondary'.

The overt content of the discourse of subatomic and high-energy physics rests then on a type-hierarchy the content of which is fixed by a specific experimental technique, namely the production and reading of primary and secondary tracks. In the case of charged particles there is a one-step relation between track and particle, while for neutral particles at least two steps are required. In this scheme 'charge' is to be read as a dispositional property. An apparatus-world ensemble which includes charged particles affords tracks. The reading of the properties of neutral particles and of quantum 'numbers' other than charge will be correspondingly more complex but of the same dispositional structure. Tracks are Bohrian phenomena, and so, by extension, are the particles that produce them. Physics proceeds by extending the structure we have outlined to include particle-affordances as well as track-affordances amongst the dispositional properties of certain apparatus-world ensembles.

But what of the intermediate vector particles (IVPs) that mediate field interactions in quantum field theory, the virtual particles that seem to be pictured in Feynman diagrams? What would justify 'transferring' particle concepts from a picture embedded in a momentum space to one in real space and time? Could an apparatus-world ensemble in which occurred electromagnetic interactions or neutral-current interactions, etc., be said to afford IVPs in the way that say a Compton effect apparatus-world ensemble affords particles by affording their tracks? A tentative answer to these questions can be found by following the pattern of reasoning that led to the experimental project of 'finding the W and the Z particles'. In terms of models the pattern reasoning could be expressed as follows:

Step 1: the luminiferous photon serves as a source for the model of the exchange particle involved in the electromagnetic interaction. The formula

$$-ig/\hbar$$

describes the 'free' (massless) photon while the kindred formula

$$-ig/q^2$$

describes the virtual (massy) photon of the lowest quantum level of electromagnetic interaction.

Step 2: the weak interaction is mediated by a class of virtual particles, W^+, W^- and Z. These too are represented by formulae of generally photonic form.

Step 3: the virtual exchange particle comes to serve as a source for a model of a new class of free particles. This final model controls the means by which the experimental program is set up to search for them. Effectively four models are interconnected by weighted similarity relations, each serving as a source for the next.

Schematically the pattern of reasoning looks like this:

Level 1: FREE PHOTON TYPE, the model for light quanta, serves as a model for free W and Z (types) as models for the representation of some so far undiscovered high energy particle interaction.

Level 2: VIRTUAL PHOTON TYPE, the exchange model for the quantised electromagnetic interaction, serves as a model for the virtual W and Z (types), the exchange model for the quantised weak interaction.

The levels are linked through the 'modelled on' relation, described in Chapter Three, between the constituent models ('models of' relation), in that virtual photons are modelled on free photons, and free W and Z particles are modelled on the virtual variety. One link goes from the free species to the virtual species of the primary photon genus, while the other goes from the virtual species to the free. How did the team at CERN know they had found the free particles? Not from the recording of suitable primary tracks, but from secondary tracks. These tracks were such that it seemed only the assumption of some process implicating W and Z particles in the antecedent steps was tenable. A key concept here is the 'cross-section' of an interaction. This concept turns out on examination to be budgeting of particles once again. This can be made sense of philosophically by invoking our affordance treatment. The apparatus at CERN, so it turned out, did indeed have, when coupled to the world, a disposition to produce secondary tracks of the right sort. In that sense that apparatus-world ensemble afforded W and Z particles. The complex fourfold structure of models as representations, laid out above, is mediated ontologically by the fact that the four models depicting particles are subtypes of the same supertype. In Level 1 the particles *depicted* are shown in real space-time, while in Level 2, as features of the Feynman diagram, they are depicted in momentum space. The secret of quantum field theory lies in this pattern of reasoning to the analysis of which we now turn.

On the walls of the church of St Cyril in Kiev two kinds of crosses are depicted. There are examples of the ordinary Christian symbol and there are also examples of the cross of Lorraine. Here are two visual images, two icons modelling very different aspects of the Christian ontology. The simple cross depicts and so represents the actual cross of Golgotha. The cross of Lorraine represents the passion of Christ, but at a second degree of abstraction. The second cross member represents the body of Jesus, but the icon represents an event and not a thing. In accordance with our general theory of representation as presented in Chapter Two the former is a visual representation while the latter is a visual metaphor. Applying this distinction to the models of quantum field theory we can see that Level 1 models are representations of the relevant affordances while Level 2 models are visual metaphors.

The formal structure on which this pattern of reasoning rests could hardly be more different from the old hypothetico-deductive pattern proposed by the logicists. Nor could the Sneed-Stegmüller way of presenting theories as sets of models work either. Quantum field theory postdates the creation of the pattern of models, and as we have shown, there is a strong ontological constraint on the permissible models, even in momentum space. It makes sense only when seen as the overt presentation of part of a type-hierarchy. The ontology of contemporary physics, in accordance with which all theorising proceeds, can be presented as a 'great' hierarchy (Figure 8.2).

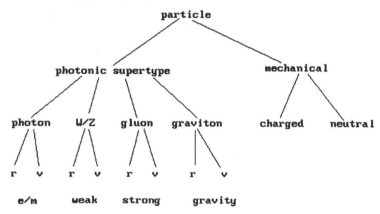

Figure 8.2. The general particle type-hierarchy

In each case the 'particle' ancestry of the real and the virtual subtypes of the photonic types reappears in the actual work of physicists as visual representation and visual metaphor respectively.

With all this in place the attribution of a secondary track affordance to the appropriate and hideously expensive apparatus/world ensemble becomes intelligible, and the project of looking for the right sort of primary tracks rational.

CHAPTER NINE

The Intersection of Metaphysics and Epistemology

1. The argument that would establish realism

The question of what the concepts of verisimilitude, plausibility and truth mean must be distinguished from the question of how we know that one theory is nearer the truth than another. Our argument in the preceding chapters has been directed to making sense of the basic concepts that must go into specifying a version of the doctrine of realism strong enough to capture the intuitions of the scientific community, yet one which is capable of being defended against the most determined of sceptics. This led us to the idea of the plausibility of a theory, as the expression of a moment in the development of a theory-family. A theory is plausible when two conditions are satisfied. It must be capable of yielding more or less correct predictions and retrodictions, the familiar criterion of 'empirical adequacy'. We could call this a 'logical' criterion. But it must also be the case that the content of the theory is based on a model which is type-wise drawn from a chunk of a type-hierarchy which expresses the common ontology accepted by the community. We could call this an 'ontological' criterion. As we have shown, the concept of plausibility admits of degrees. A theory may be more or less empirically adequate with respect to some other theory, and it may be more or less ontologically adequate in so far as the types under which its models fall are more or less similar to the types of entities of the known world. This assessment too must be made with respect to the ontological adequacy of some other theory. We shall argue that, taken together, increasing empirical adequacy and increasing ontological adequacy are inductive grounds for a claim of increasing verisimilitude, as we have defined it. In short, increasing plausibility is an inductive ground for increasing verisimilitude. It is this argument that we must set out and defend. That is the nub of the realist position. In short, now that we have shown what verisimilitude must be we must go on to show how we can know that one theory has a greater degree of verisimilitude than another. We claim that we can know this by comparing the relative plausibility of the two theories in question. If we can know this we can know whether a science has progressed and/or is currently progressing.

The two pillars of realism are very different and require different kinds of defence. The question of the semantics for the main working concepts, such as verisimilitude and truth, is a problem for philosophers. It has to be settled analytically. We believe we have shown that there is a coherent account of the meaning of the relevant concepts in the context of science. But the question of the epistemology of the applications of the now clarified concepts is a problem for historians. We have to show, empirically, that of two theories active in some domain, that which is the more plausible is closer to the truth.

2. The semantic basis of realism summarised

We have taken for granted throughout our discussion that no clear sense can be given to the idea of degrees of propositional truth. If 'correspondence' is interpreted as a relation between a statement and the state of affairs it describes, we do not see how the concepts of truth and falsity could admit of degrees. If a statement is not quite right it is surely false. But the concept of verisimilitude is just the idea of truth *likeness*. It follows that verisimilitude cannot be defined in terms of propositional truth. As we have argued, the reverse procedure can be made to work, that is it does make sense to define truth in terms of a prior and independent notion of verisimilitude. Things can be more or less like each other, in two different ways or perhaps we should say, at two levels. Two things of the same type can be compared as individuals. But we can also compare two things with respect to the types they severally represent. A bed is more like a table than it is like a stove. On what grounds do we say that? Just that bed and stove are instances of the type 'four-legged material thing' (which also includes horses and crocodiles among its instances, but not mosquitoes), and neither are instances of the type 'cooking equipment'. Is a bed more like a mosquito than it is like a stove? It depends on how these entities are considered with respect to types. The type pair 'things that can injure' and 'things that do not' might help to provide a type-context in which an answer to the question might be found.

We have argued that the content of a theory consists of a pair of models, ideally comprehended under a single ontological scheme: that is, both the descriptive and the explanatory model should instantiate the natural kinds drawn from the same type-hierarchy. In certain ideal cases the content of a theory consists of just one model, having both a descriptive and an explanatory application. The model or models are always embedded in a type-hierarchy. Since we can compare things with things and types of things with types of things, and these comparisons admit of degrees, we can talk sensibly of the verisimilitude of models: i.e. of the degree of similarity between a model and what it represents. We have yet to say how this is determined in the case of explanatory models: that is, in the case in which the states of affairs, causal substructures etc. that the model represents are not available for inspection. However, that question is irrelevant to the semantic question: what is meant by the verisimilitude of a theory? Our answer is that the verisimilitude of a theory is nothing other than the verisimilitude of its content: that is, of the model or pair of models of which that content consists. Considered in the form of discourses theories describe models, and in so far as these models are similar or dissimilar, in the respects fixed by the locally accepted type-hierarchy, to that which they are models of the theory can be said to be nearer or further from the truth than a rival.

A theory is plausible if it is empirically adequate: that is, on the whole permits successful predictions and retrodictions; and is ontologically adequate: that is, its model(s) are embedded in a hierarchy of established natural kinds.

We have now to set out convincing reasons for the claim that a theory which is more plausible than another is likely to be nearer the truth (in the sense of verisimilitude defined above). Let us call this the *plausibility thesis*. We shall argue that the plausibility thesis is capable of inductive proof, from empirical evidence. But there are two inductions needed. We know from the paradox of Clavius that theories are always underdetermined for truth when they are assessed only on the truth or falsity of their deductive consequences. It must be conceded that increasing empirical adequacy alone is not capable of establishing verisimilitude in our sense. Indefinitely many empirically false theories can yield the same predictions and retrodictions as a true theory. But scientists base their judgments of verisimilitude on another induction, the ontological induction, an induction over types.

3. The principle of epistemic invariance

The key to our defence of our revised form of convergent realism is the idea that realism can be open to test by experimental considerations. The trick is to convert the data from history and from thought experiments into the evidence to be used in an inductive argument for realism that does not beg the question. In order to do so, however, we must supplement the induction with another principle, one which we believe the anti-realist cannot possible deny, viz. the principle of epistemic invariance:

> When it comes to gathering evidence for our beliefs, *the epistemological situation remains the same for observables and unobservables alike*, no matter whether we are dealing with observables, possible observables or unobservables.

Suppose we represent convergent realism as shown in Figure 9.1:

Let A stand for the way nature actually is while T stands for the way our theories depict nature. Let B denote the way nature actually behaves according to our observations and experiments and P stand for the behaviour T predicts we will observe. We can simply assign absolute values, $|T-A|$ and $|P-B|$, to each structure and use these quantities to represent convergent realism graphically (Aronson, 1990). The graph expresses a functional relationship between verisimilitude and scientific progress, i.e. scientific progress serves as a measure of the extent our theories are getting closer to the truth. In other words, the increase in accuracy of our predictions and measurements is a function of how well the models upon which the theories we use to make these predictions and measurements depict nature. While con-

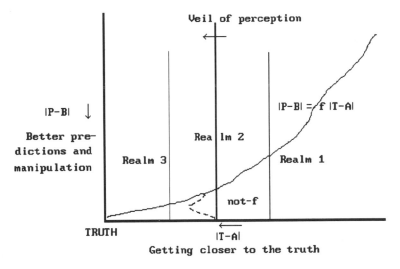

Figure 9.1. A graphical representation of convergent realism

vergent realism is not necessarily committed to using verisimilitude to *explain* scientific progress, it is committed to the view
that there is a functional *relationship* between the two, that as
our theories are getting closer to the truth we are reducing the
error of our predictions and measurements *and vice versa*. By
way of contrast the anti-realist holds that it is a real possibility
for |T-A| to increase while |P-B| decreases (dotted line on the
graph).

There are mechanics on call-in radio shows where things like
this actually happen. For example, on the 'Car Talk' show, which
can be heard on National Public Radio in the United States, the
caller gives the mechanics the year and make of the car and the
symptoms. They, in turn, suggest that the caller tries to make
certain observations and certain manipulations. On the basis of
the results, the radio mechanics 'bet' what is wrong with the car,
give an estimate of repair costs, all of this being open to future
confirmation by the caller's mechanic (Aronson, 1988).

Notice that, according to this representation, each successive
theory can be false while getting closer to the truth. In addition
to this, the functional relationship between verisimilitude and
progress may be stochastic in nature. For example, it may

exhibit a random walk but one which approaches 0 in the long run.

Using the vertical line XY to represent the 'veil of perception and the boundaries of manipulation' we can represent the principle of epistemic invariance in terms of a symmetry principle:

> The functional relationship between | P-B | and | T-A | will remain invariant as the veil of perception shifts to the right on the graph. In other words, the relationship between theory and prediction, on the one hand, and between nature and the way it behaves, on the other, remains the same as we move from observables to possible observables, from possible observables to unobservables in principle (Aronson, 1990).

We do not think there is anything controversial about this claim unless the anti-realist is prepared to defend the view that nature as we observe it behaves in a radically different fashion from that realm of nature which is unobservable *to us*. Putting problematic interpretations of quantum mechanics aside, what difference could there be between these two worlds, except the trivial one that one is observable while the other is not?

4. The induction over particulars

Sometimes it is helpful to express the structure of an argument in syllogistic form. The famous deductive-nomological theory of scientific explanation is the usual format for displaying the philosophically important features of prediction and retrodiction, successful and not so successful. In so far as the empirical adequacy of theories is tested deductive-nomologically the format has the structure of an Aristotelian syllogism of the form AII. The A premise (All metals are conductors) expresses a relevant law, the I premise the particular conditions of experimentation or observation (This is a metal wire) and the I conclusion the expected results of the test (This wire is a conductor). It is just because of the particularity of the minor premise and of the conclusion that this argument format is inductive.

Each case of a successful test of empirical adequacy establishes that certain particulars are as we supposed they were. If it is claimed that the more a theory shows itself to be empirically adequate the nearer the truth it is, it is necessary to remind ourselves of the ontology of this claim. The truth, this sense, that a sequence of better and better theories approaches is no more than the positivist's universe of correlated particulars. What about the causal substructures which the theory seems to be describing? They can appear nowhere in the induction from improving empirical adequacy to greater verisimilitude.

5. The induction over types

There is quite another sense in which theories are tested. They are also assessed for type-adequacy. This kind of test has been remarked on by philosophers for decades (including ourselves). But its importance could not be appreciated until the development of the ontology of type-hierarchies. A model and its subject are, in general, related as instantiations of two subtypes under a common supertype. The shorter the 'distance' of each from their common node, the more similar their instantiations must be. Theories are tested for type-adequacy by comparisons between their models and the reality those models represent. But if we need models to represent unknown aspects of the world how can we compare a model and its subject, a virtual world with the real one? There is a very important branch of experimental science devoted to the project of bringing to light, *under the guidance of the model*, that which the model was invented to represent. In this kind of experimentation theories are assessed for type-adequacy.

Let us call the unknown subjects of explanatory models the unexamined substructure of the world. Something can be unexamined because as a matter of fact no one has looked into it. Let us call this condition of the substructure 'accidently unexaminable' and the entity in question 'accidently unexamined'. Were there or were there not temperature inversions in tropical lakes? (And our enquiry is dated 1985.) Or it may be that at the moment no one knows how to carry out an examination, though it seems possible in principle. Were there or were there not micro-organisms implicated in anthrax? (And our enquiry is dated 1870.) Let us call this condition of the substructure 'contingently unexaminable' and the entity in question 'contingently unexamined'. Finally something may be unexamined because it seems that in principle no human being, however well equipped, could carry out an examination. Are there or are there not three quarks bound into every proton? (And our enquiry is dated 1992.) Let us call this condition of the substructure 'necessarily unexaminable' and the entity in question 'necessarily unexamined'. We finish up then with an *Umwelt* the margin of which can be divided into three loosely bounded regions: the accidentally unexamined, the contingently unexamined and the necessarily unexamined.

To set up our argument properly we must add a further distinction. The pursuit of science has always involved two main ways of acquainting ourselves with the world. We can examine something by looking at it intently, or touching or tasting or smelling it, in short by observing it. We can also examine something by manipulating it. A doctor can diagnose eczema by looking closely at the affected patch of skin, or diabetes by tasting the urine. But appendicitis is usually diagnosed by palpating the stomach and manipulating the swollen organ. In general it is possible to manipulate a broader spectrum of entities than can be observed. However, in both cases the examination involves subsumption of the entity in question under a type in a type-hierarchy: that is, it involves an assumption about its natural kind. It is quite typical of the natural sciences to construct the models that form the content of theories, which, at the time the relevant theory was formulated, cannot be compared with the realities they represent. This is for the simple reason that their subjects – that is the substructures and entities they are introduced to represent – cannot be examined.

We argue as follows: the history of science has shown that in the case of accidentally unexaminable substructures the strategy of aiming at the most plausible theory has led to increasing verisimilitude, as a matter of ascertainable fact. We can make this claim because the unexaminable substructures have, in the vast majority of cases been examined, and our strategy has proved sound. These successes support the further thesis that successful manipulation of that which was once unobserved, guided by the model, is good ground for expecting that when we get round to examining the unexamined substructure it will turn out to resemble the model: that is, the theory was near to the truth. By adding a rival theory to our story we can readily introduce the necessary comparative judgments of verisimilitude.

The next step is to apply the results of this argument to the case of the contingently unexaminable causal substructures and to run it through in just the same way. The history of science shows that, in the case of these substructures too, the strategy of aiming at the greatest empirical and ontological adequacy – that is, at the most plausible theory – has led to increasing verisimilitude. Technical advances, such as the microscope and the radio telescope, make that which was previously unexaminable examinable. But this can, and usually does, occur in two stages. Guided by their model, scientists can usually manipulate the causal substructure and the 'hidden' entities represented by the model, before they can observe them. Successful manipulation, we argue, has been shown to support a claim to greater verisimilitude, which has been substantiated by later technical advances permitting the beings in question to be observed. Boyle argued for the reality of corpuscles on the grounds that the techniques of chemistry, when closely analysed, turned out to be intelligible only as ways of manipulating the unobservable corpuscularian substructures of material stuff. We can now say that ultramicroscopes, electron microscopes, X-ray diffraction equipment and so on have inductively supported Boyle's claim, by making observable what for Boyle was only manipulable. Once again the key is the achievement of ontological adequacy by choosing a type for one's models from the relevant branch or chunk of a type-hierarchy. But that observation leads to the next step. The more that the strategy of picking one's models from just *this* hierarchy of natural kinds pays off for verisimilitude the more we are justified in taking that hierarchy to be truly representative of the type structure of the natural world.

6. The final step: betting on 'truth'

The final step in our argument for the type induction to scientific realism as we have defined it is to extend the procedure to those theories whose models represent causal substructures, entities, processes and so on that are unexaminable in principle. The key to the extension lies in the important distinction between manipulation of the substructure guided by the model and the observation of typical entities of that substructure. There is an empirical method for ontological testing that lies between imagining a model and observing an object. It is the method of manipulation. It is so commonplace that we are hardly aware of its ubiquitous role in our lives and practice. Every time we turn on the shower *and stand underneath it* we are, in effect, using the unobservable gravitational field to manipulate the water. The way that Stern and Gerlach manipulated magnetic fields to manipulate atomic nuclei in their famous apparatus is metaphysically much the same as our everyday strategy of standing under the shower. Let us turn to the substructures of our third kind, the necessarily unexaminable. It turns out that it is only with reference to observation that they are outside our ken. They are not unexaminable if we take account of Boyle's important observation that much that we cannot observe we can manipulate. The force of this step for our inductive argument for realism is overwhelming. It completely eliminates that form of scepticism that casts doubt on our right to believe in the existence of subatomic particles, fields, and indeed most of our basic categories of beings. They would not figure in our common ontologies at all were they wholly unmanipulable.

Let us finally tie down as precisely as possible what this last step involves. It is an induction over types of types. We have argued that it is a matter of fact that the pursuit of plausibility in our formulation of theories has paid off in increasing verisimilitude, despite one or two cases where things went awry. Our argument, we wish to remind the reader, is inductive. But that induction involves the principle that increasingly successful manipulation as guided by the model is a good ground for a claim for verisimilitude, that is for an increasingly good match between the model and what it represents, the causal substructure, etc. This principle, we claim, is provable inductively for the first two kinds of cases, those in which the subjects of our models are accidentally and contingently unexaminable. This principle links model-guided manipulative success with verisimilitude of the model. We can leave out the 'observation' link from this point on. We have established inductively that there is a direct link between manipulability and verisimilitude. And that is what we need for claims of verisimilitude for models in use in such branches of physics as nuclear theory and quantum field theory. But we must now bring in the induction over types. The history of science, we claim, not only justifies our strategies of aiming at plausibility in theory formation, but also our continued use of chunks of the type-hierarchy of natural kinds, forged in the centuries of scientific development, that has served us so well and survived so many ontological assessments. It is by reference to that induction that we can boldly fill the observationally empty space of our *Umwelt* with charges, fields and particles, in the certain hope of successfully manipulating them (Aronson, 1988, 1990).

The anti-realist still has one reply available. In the examples cited the scientists who take the success of their manipulations as inductive evidence for the verisimilitude of the type-hierarchies with which they control their equipment know very well what kinds of individuals they are postulating. But this is not the case for those truly unobservable objects (if indeed the category of 'object' can be used of them at all) that are modelled in high-energy physics, cosmology and so on. The induction is a bad one because the samples were biased. There is no guarantee that the ontologies with which scientists have successfully worked until now are any guide to those that will accurately depict the denizens of regions of the world of which we have never had any observable instances.

We have two answers to the above protest. In the first place, it is not at all clear that, just because one is extrapolating from known because observable types of objects to unobservable types of entities, the relationship between better prediction, more manipulability and getting closer to the truth can be called into question. This is what the principle of epistemic invariance, cited in the earlier sections of this chapter, is concerned with. Again, the induction is carried over types of types of things. The property 'being unable to be observed' is not a type of the sort relevant to planning manipulations and so on, nor is it the least plausible as a natural kind. Suppose we could construct a box which, once sealed, cannot be reopened. We place an object in a normal box and an object of the same type (T) in the sealed box. Two scientists perform experiments on the objects in the boxes by sending the same input signals into the boxes. It does not surprise us to learn that they receive the same outputs. Why should we question the reliability of the inference of the second scientist to the existence of an object of type T in the sealed box but not the identical conclusion drawn by the first, *just because the latter object is no longer an observable?*

The example can be extended to come closer to the kind of situation with which one is faced, say, in quark theory. There is a way to perform these 'sealed-box' experiments which makes the above criticism simply irrelevant by guaranteeing that all the 'objects' are of types previously unknown to the experimenter. All we have to do is to utilise the virtual world experiments that were depicted in Chapter Seven. Instead of using objects that exist in the actual world to populate our sealed boxes, and the laws we know they obey to make ontological inferences from what we see to be the reactions of the boxes to our treatments, we create virtual worlds, each one with its own set of objects and laws. The behaviour of the beings in each virtual world will result in changes in 'observables', changes that show up on the graphic display of the computer within which our virtual worlds are created. But each virtual world will have 'unobservable' states of its constituent entities that are never displayed on the screen.

Our sealed box experiments will now look like this. We generate a long list of virtual worlds, each with its own set of objects and laws. Use a random number generator to select a large number of such worlds from the original catalogue. From the behaviour of objects on the graphic display, the experimenter is to formulate hypotheses about the world underlying observations of the virtual world. On the basis of these hypotheses, the experimenter predicts new displays on the screen of the computer corresponding to new 'experimental results'. Again, we are only interested in successful predictions. Take the cases of successful predictions and see if they are based on hypotheses and theories that are closer to the truth, as measured by the Tversky formula, to which we have referred in Chapter Two.

The realist need not claim that 100 per cent of the cases of better predictions and increased manipulation result from truer hypotheses. All that is required is that the 'curve of scientific progress' be a random walk which gets closer to the truth in our sense – that is involves models of the world of greater and greater verisimilitude – in the long run (Aronson, 1990).

*

It is no part of our position to claim that a defensible version of scientific realism must be based on a universal thesis of uniform and increasing verisimilitude, without let or hindrance. Inductive hypotheses are easier to establish if they are not expressed as universal claims. For example, the hypothesis that 99 per cent of the crow population is black is more easily confirmed than that 100 per cent are black. The latter hypothesis has no confidence intervals – no standard deviations. To assess it we are forced to use the straight-line rule. One white crow disconfirms it utterly. The former hypothesis, on the other hand, does allow us to adjust the confidence level to our degree of confidence we have about the relationship between better predictions, manipulations and verisimilitude. In our imaginary example, if 80 per cent of a sample of 1000 cases of better predictions and more successful manipulations turned out to be based on more verisimilitudinous models, then we can be confident to the 0.1 level that these results did not occur by chance. It is this induction that carries us from those cases in which the boxes that were once thought to be firmly sealed (those that contained viruses, for instance) were opened and found to contain more or less what the scientific community expected in those sealed boxes which at this time we believe we will never open. Thus if our 80 per cent are drawn from the initial segment of the sequence, since the induction is over a finite population, we can always compute the confidence level that obtains at this moment. However, we can see that the above experiments would make no sense according to the old version of verisimilitude, which was expressed in terms of the balance struck between correspondences and mismatches. All we need to claim is that while the world the scientists in some team hypothesise is not exactly the same as the virtual world they were assigned, it was nevertheless more similar to it than the ones they rejected.

References

Armstrong, D. 1978 *Universals and Scientific Realism*, vol. 1 of *A Theory of Universals* New York: Cambridge University Press

Armstrong, D. 1983 *What is a Law of Nature?* Cambridge: Cambridge University Press

Aronson, J.L. 1984 *A Realist Philosophy of Science* London: Macmillan

Aronson, J.L. 1988 'Testing for convergent realism' in A. Fine & J. Leplin (eds) *Proceedings of the 1988 Biennial Meeting of the Philosophy of Science Association* 1 188-93

Aronson, J.L. 1989 'The Bayesians and the Raven Paradox' *Nous* 23 221-40

Aronson, J.L. 1990 'Experimental realism' in R. Bhaskar (ed) *Harré and his Critics* Oxford: Blackwell, pp. 48-63

Aronson, J.L. 1991 'Verisimilitude and type-hierarchies' *Philosophical Topics* 18 5-16

Austin, J.L. 1970 *Philosophical Papers* Oxford: Oxford University Press

Bambrough, R. 1961 'Universals and family resemblances' in Loux 1970, 109-27

Bennett, J. 1974 'Counterfactuals and possible worlds' *Canadian Journal of Philosophy* 4 381-402

Bhaskar, R. 1973 *A Realist Theory of Science* Brighton: Harvester

Black, M. 1962 *Models and Metaphors* Ithaca, N.Y.: Cornell University Press

Black, M. 1979 'More about metaphor' in A. Ortony (ed) *Metaphor and Thought* Cambridge: Cambridge University Press, pp. 19-43

Bohr, N. 1958 *Atomic Physics and Human Knowledge* New York: Wiley

Boscovich, R.J. 1763 (1966) *A Theory of Natural Philosophy* Venice (Boston: MIT Press)

Boyd, R. 1984 'The current status of scientific realism' in J. Leplin (ed) *Scientific Realism* Berkeley: University of California Press

Boyd, R. 1990 'Realism, conventionality and "realism about" ' in G. Boolos (ed) *Festschrift for Hilary Putnam* Cambridge: Cambridge University Press, pp. 171-95

Boyd, R. 1991 'Realism, anti-foundationalism and the enthusiasm for natural kinds' *Philosophical Studies* 161 127-48

Bridge, J. 1977 *Beginning Model Theory* Oxford: Oxford University Press

Brown, H.R. & Harré, R. 1990 *Philosophical Foundations of Quantum Field Theory* Oxford: Oxford University Press

Campbell, N.R. 1920 (1957) *Physics: The Elements* (reprinted as *The Foundations of Physics* New York: Dover)

Devitt, M. 1984 *Realism and Truth* Princeton: Princeton University Press

Diedrich, W. 1989 'The development of Marx's economic theory' *Erkenntnis* **30** 147-64

Del Rey, G. 1974 'Current problems and perspectives in MO-LCAO theory of molecules' *Advances in Quantum Chemistry* **8** 95-136

Dretske, F. 1977 'The laws of nature' *Philosophy of Science* **44** 248-68

Eddington, A. 1929 *The Nature of the Physical World* Cambridge: Cambridge University Press

Enc, B. 1976 'Reference of theoretical terms' *Nous* **10** 261-82

Etchemedy, J. 1988 'Models, semantics and logical truth' *Linguistic Philosophy* **11** 91-106

Fahlman, S.E. 1979 *NETL: A System for Representing and Using Real World Knowledge* Cambridge, Mass.: MIT Press

Fales, E. 1982 'Generic universals' *Australian Journal of Philosophy* **60:1** 29-39

Frege, G. 1892 'On sense and reference' in M. Black (trans) *Translations from the Philosophical Writings of Gottlob Frege* Oxford: Blackwell

Gati, I. & Tversky, A. 1984 'Weighting common and distinctive features in perceptual and conceptual judgments' *Cognitive Psychology* **16** 341-70

Gibson, J.J. 1979 *The Ecological Approach to Human Perception* Boston: Howard Mifflin

Giere, R. 1985 'Constructive realism' in P.M. Churchland & C.A. Hooker (eds) *Images of Science* Chicago: Chicago University Press

Giere, R. 1988 *Explaining Science* Chicago: Chicago University Press

Gleick, J. 1987 *Chaos: Making a New Science* New York: Penguin

Goffman, E. 1964 *The Presentation of Self in Everyday Life* Harmondsworth: Penguin

Goffman, E. 1969 *Where the Action Is* Harmondsworth: Penguin

Goodman, N. 1965 *Fact, Fiction and Forecast* Indianapolis: Bobbs-Merrill

Greene, R. 1727 *The Principles of the Philosophy of the Expansive and Attractive Forces* Cambridge

Hacking, I. 1991 'A tradition of natural kinds' *Philosophical Studies* **161** 1991

Harré, R. 1973 *The Principles of Scientific Thinking* London: Macmillan

Harré, R. 1986 *Varieties of Realism* Oxford: Blackwell

Harré, R. 1988 'Where models and analogies really count' *International Studies in the Philosophy of Science* **2:2** 118-33

Harré, R. & Madden, E.H. 1977 *Causal Powers* Oxford: Blackwell

Hautamaki, A. 1986 'Points of view and their logical analysis' *Acta Philosophica Fennica* **41**

Hertz, H. 1894 *The Principles of Mechanics* (reprint) New York: Dover

Hesse, M. 1961 *Models and Analogies in Science,* London: Sheed and Ward

Hesse, M. 1980 *Revolutions and Reconstructions in the Philosophy of Science* Bloomington: Indiana University Press

Hesse, M. 1988 'Theories, family resemblances and analogy' in D. Helman (ed) *Analogical Reasoning* Dordrecht: Kluwer

Hesse, M. 1993 'Models, metaphors and truth' in F.R. Ankersmit & J.J.A. Mooij (eds) *Metaphor and Knowledge* Dordrecht: Kluwer forthcoming

Honner, J. 1987 *The Description of Nature* Oxford: Clarendon Press

Hume, D. 1739 *A Treatise of Human Nature* London. Book I, Parts II and III.

Hume, D. 1748 *An Enquiry Concerning Human Understanding* London

Jackson, F. 1977 'A causal theory of counterfactuals' *Australasian Journal of Philosophy* **55** 3-21

Jackson, F. 1991 (ed) *Conditionals* Oxford: Oxford University Press

Johnson, W.E. 1921 *Logic* Cambridge: Cambridge University Press

Kant, I. 1786 (1970) *The Metaphysical Foundations of Natural Science* trans J. Ellington. Riga (Indianapolis: Indiana University Press)

Keil, F.C. 1979 *Semantic and Conceptual Development: An Ontological Perspective* Cambridge, Mass: Harvard University Press

Keil, F.C. 1981 'Constraints on knowledge and cognitive development' *Psychological Review* **88** 197-227

Keil, F.C. 1989 *Concepts, Kinds and Cognitive Development* Cambridge, Mass.: MIT Press

Korner, S. 1959 'On determinables and resemblances' in *The Aristotelian Society for the Systematic Study of Philosophy*, Part I, Supplementary volume **33** 25-40

Kuipers, Theo. A.F. forthcoming 'Naive and refined truth approximation' *Synthèse*

Lakoff, G. & Johnson, M. (1980) *Metaphors We Live By* Chicago: Chicago University Press

Laudan, L. 1981 'A confutation of convergent realism' *Philosophy of Science* **48** 19-49

Lewis, D. 1973 *Counterfactuals* Cambridge, Mass.: Harvard University Press

Lewis, D. 1991 'Counterfactual dependence' in Jackson (1991) 46-75

Locke, J. 1690 (1961) *An Essay Concerning Human Understanding* ed J.W. Yolton. London: Dent

Loux, M.J. (ed) 1970 *Universals and Particulars: Readings in Ontology* Garden City, New York: Anchor Books

Margolis, J. 1985 *Science without Foundations* Oxford: Blackwell

Marsh, P., Rosser, E. & Harré, R. 1977 *The Rules of Disorder* London: Routledge and Kegan Paul

Medin, D.L. & Shoben, E.J. 1988 'Context and structure in conceptual combination' *Cognitive Psychology* **20** 158-90

Medin, D.L. 1989 'Concepts and conceptual structure' *American Psychologist* **44** 1469-81

207   *References*

Mendelsohn, E. 1987 *Introduction to Mathematical Logic* (3rd edition) Monterey: Wadsworth, p. 48

Miller, D. 1978 'The distance between constituents' *Synthèse* **38** 197-212

Mondadori, F. & Morton, A. 1979 'Modal realism: the poisoned pawn' in M.J. Loux (ed) *The Possible and the Actual* Ithaca, N.Y.: Cornell University Press, pp. 235-52

Murphy, G.L. & Medin, D.L. 1985 'The role of theories in conceptual coherence' *Psychological Review* **92** 289-316

Newton-Smith, W. 1981 *The Rationality of Science* London: Routledge and Kegan Paul

Newton-Smith, W. 1990 'Modest realism' *International Studies in the Philosophy of Science* 4 17-26

Ninniluoto, I. 1987 *Truthlikeness* Dordrecht: Reidel

Oddie, G. 1986 'The poverty of the Popperian program for truthlikeness' *Philosophy of Science* **53** 163-78

Pearse, D. 1981 'Is there a theoretical justification for a non-statement view of theories?' *Synthese* **46** 1-39

Peterson, I. 1991 'Cracks in the cosmos' *Science News* **139** 344-6

Popper, K.R. 1972 *Objective Knowledge* Oxford: Clarendon Press

Prior, A.N. 1949 'Determinables, determinates and determinants' *Mind* **58** 1-20

Putnam, H. 1983 *Realism and Reason* Cambridge: Cambridge University Press

Putnam, H. 1984 'What is realism?' in J. Leplin (ed) *Scientific Realism* Berkeley: University of California Press

Redhead, M. 1980 'The use of models in physics' *British Journal for the Philosophy of Science* **31** 145-63

Roberts, L. 1986 'The figure ground model for the explanation of the determination of indexical reference' *Synthèse* **68** 441-86

Rundle, B.B. 1990 *Wittgenstein and Contemporary Philosophy of Language* Oxford: Blackwell

Santema, J.H. 1978 *Modellen in de Wetenskape en de Trepassing Epienen* Delft: Delft University Press

Schillp, P. 1949 (ed) *Albert Einstein: philosopher-scientist* New York: Harper and Brothers

Searle, J. 1959 'On determinables and resemblances' in *The Aristotelian Society for the Systematic Study of Philosophy*, Part II, Supplementary volume **33** 141-58

Searle, J. 1967 'Determinables and determinates' in P. Edwards (ed) *The Encyclopedia of Philosophy* New York: Macmillan & The Free Press

Searle, J. 1979 'Metaphor' in A. Ortony (ed) *Metaphor and Thought*, Cambridge: Cambridge University Press, pp. 92-123

Shastri, L. 1988 *Semantic Networks: An Evidential Formalisation and its Connectionist Realisation* San Mateo: Morgan Kaufmann

Sloate, M.A. 1978 'Time in counterfactuals' *Philosophical Review* **87** 3-27

Smith, E.E. 1989 'Concepts and Induction' in I.M. Posner (ed) *Foundations of Cognitive Science* Cambridge, Mass., pp. 501-26

Sneed, T. 1974 *The Logical Structure of Mathematical Physics* Dordrecht: Reidel

Sowa, J.F. 1987 'Semantic networks' in E. Shapiro (ed) *Encyclopedia of Artificial Intelligence* New York: John Wiley

Stebbing, L.S. 1937 *Philosophy and the Physicists* London: Methuen

Stegmüller, W. 1976 *The Structure and Dynamics of Theories* New York: Springer Verlag

Stegmüller, W. 1979 *The Structural View of Theories* Berlin and New York: Springer Verlag, pp. 27-8

Swoyer, C. 1982 'The nature of natural law' *Australian Journal of Philosophy* **60**

Tichy, P. 1976 'Verisimilitude redefined' *British Journal for the Philosophy of Science* **27** 25-42

Toulmin, S.E. 1956 *The Philosophy of Science* London: Hutchinson

Tversky, A. 1977 'Features of similarity' *Psychological Review* **84:4** 327-52

van Fraasen, B. 1980 *The Scientific Image* Oxford: Oxford University Press

Vetter, H. 1977 'A new concept of verisimilitude' *Theory and Decision* **8** 369-75

Vision, G. 1988 *Modern Anti-realism and Manufactured Truth* London: Routledge

Waismann, F. 1947 'Verifiability' in A. Flew (ed) 1960 *Logic and Language*, first series, Oxford: Blackwell

Waismann, F. 1968 *How I See Philosophy* London: Macmillan

Way, E.C. 1991 *Knowledge Representation and Metaphor* Dordrecht: Kluwer

Wilder, R.L. 1952 *Introduction to the Foundations of Mathematics* New York: John Wiley

Wittgenstein, L. 1953 *Philosophical Investigations* Oxford: Blackwell

Woods, L.C. 1977 'Maxwell's models', Address to the New South Wales Institute of Technology

Woods, W.A. 1975 'What's in a link: foundations for semantic networks' in D.G. Bobrow & A.M. Collins (eds) *Representation and Understanding: Studies in Cognitive Science* New York: Academic Press

Wylie, A. 1988 ' "Simple" analogy and the role of relevancy assumptions: implications of archaeological practice' *International Studies in the Philosophy of Science* **2** 134-50

Index of Names

Subject Index